YOU'RE HIRED! JOB INTERVIEW PREPARATION

JOB SEARCH STRATEGIES THAT WORK

RAE A. STONEHOUSE

Live For Excellence Productions

Rae A. Stonehouse
Author & Publishing Consultant
publishing@live4excellence.com

#9 Second Drive
Kelowna, BC
live4excellence.com

COPYRIGHT

～

E-book - ISBN: 978-1-9994754-2-0
Print - ISBN: 978-1-9994754-5-1

Live For Excellence Productions
1221 Velrose Drive
Kelowna, B.C., Canada
V1X6R7
https://liveforexcellence.com

CONNECT WITH US

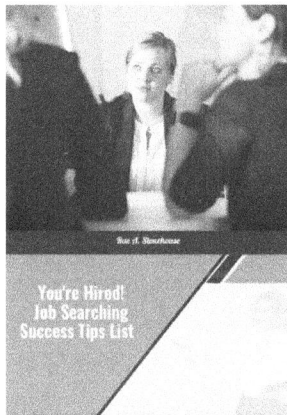

Subscribe to our **You're Hired! Job Search Strategies That Work Newsletter** to receive job searching sage advice from Rae A. Stonehouse and receive **You're Hired! Job Searching Success Tips List**, a free e-book providing you with 55 tips to landing your next job.

http://eepurl.com/ghp73f

Visit us on the web at http://yourehirednow.com.

Check out our **Jobs Now Blog** @ http//yourehirednow.com for job searching advice to frequently asked questions.

For even more job searching tips & techniques, join us on Facebook https://www.facebook.com/jobstrategiesthatwork/

Twitter: https://twitter.com/yourehirednow

1. WELCOME!

H i there! Welcome to **You're Hired! Job Interview Preparation - Job Search Strategies That Work.**

Make no mistake. Searching for work... is work!

It takes time, effort and a lot of self-motivation to succeed in your search.

While you have your skills and experience in place to apply for and land your dream job, or one that leads you to it, searching for a job requires a whole different set of skills.

In many job markets being invited for an interview can be like winning a lottery. Your resume likely got you in the door, now you need to wow the Interviewer and do your best in the interview to land the job.

This book focuses on *job interview preparation strategies* to maximize your job searching effectiveness and is excerpted and expanded upon, from my book **You're Hired! Job Search Strategies That Work.**

Nobody can make a promise if you follow their program, you will be guaranteed the results you are looking for and I won't either.

I

However, I'm confident if you follow the strategies outlined in this book, your chances of being successful in landing a job are increased.

From my experience, one of the biggest problems job seekers often face is they feel they are coming from an inferior position and they don't have a lot of personal power. The belief being the Employer has the superior position and has all the power.

Yes, they have the job and they have the power to give you the job ... or not.

What you may not realize is many Hiring Managers are under similar pressures as you, the job seeker. They have the pressure of finding the right candidate for the vacancy they need to fill.

They are accountable to their superiors should the person they hire not work out. It has been said an inappropriate hire can cost the organization an additional 30 to 50 percent over the job position's annual wage. This would include lost productivity incurred when the new hire is oriented, the cost of advertising for new applicants and the time taken to interview and follow up with applicants.

Hiring managers are under pressure to hire the right candidate.

Your task is to become the *only* choice. The *right* choice!

As I mentioned earlier, we are likely not experts at searching for jobs and landing one. It isn't something we do on a regular basis.

As I researched the content for my book **You're Hired! Job Search Strategies That Work**, I found the problem is compounded by a lack of hard facts on what are the best-practices for job searching.

I'm reminded of an old parable about a group of blind men who were required to touch an elephant and to describe their observations.

Each one felt a different part, but only one part, such as a tusk or the trunk. When they compared notes, they learned they were in complete disagreement.

I found the same to be true when researching strategic job searching skills.

Each webpage from my search results on the internet spoke from the perspective of the writer whether they were a resume writer, an Employer Hiring Manager, recruiter, etc.

Much the same as the blind men describing what an elephant looks like, their advice is from their perspective. That makes sense to me. We all create our own reality. My reality is completely different from anyone else's.

The problem is the job search 'experts' state their observations as hard facts. They believe what they write is true. And then the next article you read, will dispute what the first expert had said and they will present their truths.

How can something be both true and false at the same time? You must never do this. You must always do this.

Same advice. Can something be both yes and no?

I don't consider myself an expert at job searching.

What I am very good at though is taking subjects people struggle with, finding better, easier ways to do things and breaking it down to basic strategies that work.

I create *systems* to solve *problems*.

Years ago, I moved my family across Canada to a city where I didn't know anyone.

I had a brand-new home built for me, but I didn't have a job waiting for me when I got there.

At the time, the new location was very hostile towards people who had moved from the east to the west coast.

I often heard "you Easterners come out here and steal our jobs…"

I found jobs were limited. I found getting an interview for a position I had applied for was like winning a lottery.

I also found my new geographical area had what they called a 'Sunshine Tax.'

As a desirable place to live, the cost of living is higher and employers believe they can get away with paying their employees lower wages. The idea being you the worker should be grateful to have a job and the employer can get away with paying you less.

'If you don't want the job, somebody else will!"

I got so tired of hearing about stealing local jobs I started to change my story when I attended local business networking events.

Instead of saying I was *unemployed*, I would say I had *retired* early.

I was 39 years old and the illusion I had retired early seem to resolve the 'you Easterners' complaint.

However, I used to add "if the right job came along, I would likely consider going back to work."

It was offered somewhat tongue in cheek.

It took me a good six months to land a job. It wasn't as good a job as I had hoped.

It was a compromise until something better came along.

I describe my employment experience at my new location as being like a roller coaster ride.

I went from being unemployed, to employed. I went from not getting enough hours to getting too many.

I went from being employed to being laid off.

I went from being employed to being self-employed.

Self-employment ended when I came back from a vacation to find my only client had sold their business i.e. a vocational school and the new owners had no idea who I was or had need of my services.

Back to being unemployed.

Then I got a job in another city. It was a 90-mile round trip, daily.

I went from being at the employer's beck and call for three years working as many hours as I could as a casual staff. Then I got fired!

Then I got *unfired* and a new job, same company, a few blocks away.

I went from full time to no time to part time to even more part time. Then less time and even less time.

I had to tell my manager I couldn't afford to stay and I couldn't afford to go.

We solved the problem by me picking up hours from another worker who wanted to work less.

The downside is I work a lot of night shifts and it is still a 90 mile, 150-kilometre round trip for work.

I think you can see why I call it a roller coaster ride.

Over the years, I have been invited to numerous job search training programs as a guest speaker, promoting the value of public speaking skills to the job search and interviewing process as well as networking skills.

Throughout this book, I will be providing you with what I consider to be best practices for preparing for a job interview.

Some content may disagree with what the so-called experts would say but then again... the next one would likely agree with me.

If you are a sports fan, you will recognize that any sport has a set of rules and varying degrees of competition.

Searching for a job, your job, is a competitive situation.

It could come down to two or more possible candidates, hopefully you, being one of them, having very similar credentials and qualifications.

If there was ever a time self-promotional skills and self-confidence would come into play, it would be in the job searching and interviewing process.

Being able to effectively promote yourself can make the difference between landing the job and a "thank you very much, but we won't be hiring you at this time."

WELCOME ABOARD AND I HOPE YOU ENJOY OUR JOURNEY TOGETHER!

~

SECTION ONE: INTRODUCTION TO JOB INTERVIEWING

2. THE INITIAL PHONE CALL

Y our resume wowed them! They want to speak with you in person. Now what?

The interview process starts from the *very first* phone call the prospective employer makes to you to arrange for an interview.

Be prepared! You are being judged!

If you aren't available to take a phone call *live and in person*, your telephone answering machine, yes, some people still do have them or your voice mail, should have an *appropriate, professional* sounding greeting. When you are job searching, it isn't the time to have a catchy novelty telephone greeting.

Have pen & paper at the ready.

Have easy access to your personal agenda or commitments so you can readily arrange for an interview appointment. Be prepared to ask them some quick questions in return.

Questions You Need to Ask:

Here are some questions to ask while you have them on the phone or in an e-mail if that was their initial contact method:

- time & location?
- who will be conducting the interview?
- what format will the interview be?
- are there other people being interviewed for the job? [you might want to be careful with this question though]
- is there anything you need to bring with you?

~

IN OUR NEXT CHAPTER WE LOOK AT *PREPARING* FOR YOUR FIRST interview.

3. INTRODUCTION TO THE FIRST INTERVIEW

I n an Employer's attempt to fill a staffing vacancy, they may interview *any number* of people and they may interview an individual *a number* of times before they make their mind up as to who they will hire.

This chapter addresses your first interview for a *specific* job application.

We look at some things you **should** do and some you **shouldn't**.

We look at what you should *expect* in this first interview and some suggestions on how to answer interview questions.

In *later* sections of the program, we dig even deeper into interviewing tactics and strategies.

While this chapter focuses on it being your *first* interview, you need to be aware it might be the only one the Employer plans on conducting. So, you need to do your best at every step of the interview process.

Here are some interview formats you may encounter:

Individual Interviewer - You may find yourself being interviewed by only one person.

Team Interview (panel) - In a panel interview you may face 3 or more interviewers. They will have prepared in advance a series of interview questions to ask you. As one asks you a question, the others will be scoring you on how you answer.

They will likely take turns asking you the questions. And they will have assigned a rating to each question. Upon completion of the interview they will compare scores and then *rate* you against others competing for the same job.

Team with other applicants - Team interviews can be quite challenging. You will likely be interviewed at the same time as a number of other potential candidates. You could find yourself sitting on chairs placed in a circle.

THE INTERVIEWERS WILL HAVE CREATED A NUMBER OF QUESTIONS IN advance. They likely have other criteria in mind as well as a way to determine your suitability for hire. They could be looking for how you get along with the others in the interview group.

They could be looking for *natural* leadership abilities to emerge from this group interview or even *how* you respond to pressure.

. . .

ON CAMERA - YOU COULD WALK INTO THE INTERVIEW ROOM TO FIND A camera facing you and perhaps a number of television/monitor screens with interviewers located at remote locations.

INTERVIEWS CONDUCTED ON SKYPE OR CONFERENCE CALLS ARE becoming more mainstream these days.

∾

"IT'S THE ACTION, NOT THE FRUIT OF THE ACTION THAT'S IMPORTANT. You have to do the right thing. It may not be in your power, may not be in your time, that there'll be any fruit. But that does not mean you stop doing the right thing. You may never know what results come from your action. But if you do nothing, there will be no results." -- Mahatma Gandhi

4. DRESS FOR SUCCESS

Will Rogers said, "I never met a man I didn't like."

An employment interview is a place to be liked. Unless you're likeable, you won't be hireable.

When job hunting, dress for success.

In job-hunting, first impressions are critical.

Remember, you are marketing a product -- *yourself* -- to a potential employer. And the first thing the employer sees when greeting you is your attire.

Therefore, you must make every effort to have the proper dress for the type of job you are seeking.

The old saying 'never judge a book by its cover' may be a good one, but interviewers are human like everybody else and likely to act upon their *first* impressions. So, you want to make sure you are giving a good one.

$$\approx$$

IN THE NEXT CHAPTER, WE LOOK AT HOW TO ORGANIZE YOUR presentation or responses in your upcoming interview.

5. ORGANIZING YOUR PRESENTATION

This chapter is on **Organizing Your Presentation** and offers tips on how to answer job interview questions.

You might be wondering why I'm using the term *'presentation'* at all.

I think it is helpful to think of each of your interview questions as being mini speeches or presentations.

It might seem a little out of order with this section, but the idea is you give it some thought and practice before the interview process is upon you.

Here are some sure-fire formulas of organizing your responses to the interviewer's questions.

Past, Present, Future

Here is an example ... "in the *past* I would have handled the situation this way...

Recently I experienced a similar situation and this is how I handled it.

I learned from it and here is *how* I would handle it should I encounter it again."

Here's another possible outline ... Problem/Cause/Solution

- The problem is
- The problem is caused by
- Some solutions are
- The best solution is

Let's look at an example of using the Problem cause solution outline:

"From my *perspective*, the problem seems to be blah, blah, blah."

"I *believe* it is caused by blah, blah, blah."

"From my *experience*, there are several different solutions to this problem. We could blah, blah, blah or another way might be to blah, blah, blah."

"I believe the *best* solution is to blah, blah, blah."

That last one is a different blah, blah, blah from the previous ones of course.

The idea with using this outline is you want to showcase yourself as an *expert* and you are *capable* of *independent, strategic* thinking.

DALE CARNEGIE'S MAGIC FORMULA

Before we look at his formula, some of you might be wondering who he is.

He wrote a book titled *How to Win Friends and Influence People* that was first published in 1936, it has sold over *30 million copies world-wide* and went on to be named #19 on *Time Magazine*'s list of *100 most* influential books in 2011.

His formula is **Example, Point, Reason.**

Let's look at how the formula would work.

Example: Give details of an incident that graphically illustrates your main idea.

Example: "This company has had some challenges with the people they are hiring. They keep leaving."

Point: Tell exactly what you want your audience to do.

Example: "You should hire me now and pay me a good salary so I will stay longer than the others."

Reason: Highlight the advantage or benefit to be gained when they do what you ask them to do.

Example: "I am a proven dedicated and loyal employee, with a long history of quality service and you would be stupid if you didn't hire me."

Okay, that example is quite tongue and cheek. While it is something you might love to do in an interview, I wouldn't suggest it.

However, it does illustrate example, point, reason.

Every presentation regardless of its length, should have these three components:

- Opening
- Body
- Closing

Your opening and your closing should take about 15% of your time, so a total of 30%.

The remaining of your time, 70% is the body, where you expand upon your content.

If you were delivering a speech, the opening is where you would grab your audience's attention. I call it 'wake em, up… shake em up!"

You can't quite do that when answering an interview question.

Your interviewer would probably think you are crazy if you started yelling at them. But what you can do in your opening when answering an interview question is to set the stage for the fact you actually know something about this question and you are prepared to speak about it.

As for the *body* of your answer, this is where you provide the *details* of your answer.

An effective *conclusion* to an interview question can be to do a *quick summary* of your response and something to the effect your response is over and you are ready for the next question.

~

OUR NEXT CHAPTER PROVIDES AN OVERVIEW OF THE INTERVIEWING process.

"DON'T GET COMPLACENT. PUSH YOURSELF OUT OF YOU COMFORT ZONE and set higher standards of achievement for yourself. Once you've achieved a standard of excellence, never let it rest... push yourself even higher." -- Dave Anderson

6. YOU GOT AN INTERVIEW. NOW WHAT?

L et's look at the job interview process, starting off with your first interview.

In my part of the world where we have a tight job market, just getting to the interview stage can be like winning a lottery.

Your resume likely got you to the interview stage. So, what happens now?

The goal for this first face-to-face encounter is to win a second one.

Tell yourself *beforehand* that you need to come away with a good sense of the most effective techniques and timing for this target.

Then when you are inside the prospective employer's office:

Be Observant

Throughout the interview, *look and listen* to gather information that will help you.

A successful interview requires the ability to think on your feet, metaphorically of course. You will more than likely be sitting down for your interview.

Your undivided attention is necessary to seize opportunities as they arise.

Take Out Your Well-Organized Notebook and Jot Down Notes

It makes you look professional. Write names, titles, buzzwords, products, and other items you can use in the follow up stage.

Don't reduce your eye contact with the interviewer; don't ask him or her to repeat anything or how to spell something.

You *can* and *should* ask questions. Not only do the right questions help you control the interview, but by asking them, you elicit information to fuel your follow up.

Ask the right questions. Don't ask personal controversial or negative questions of any kind. Stay away from asking anything that will lead into sensitive areas.

Invariably, salary and benefits should be avoided.

Nowadays, you can often gather quite a bit of information about the organization you are applying to by doing a search on the internet. It will be expected you have *some* understanding of their business.

While some knowledge will certainly be helpful, a *lack* of knowledge or asking questions you should already know the answers to, could work against you.

Here are examples of benign questions that may have a favorable impact:

How many employees does the company have?

What are the company's plans for expansion?

Is the business operated as a proprietorship or a non-profit?

What is the supervisor's management style?

What is the supervisor's title?

Who does the supervisor report to?

Are you ready and able to hire now?

How long will it take to make a hiring decision?

How long has the position been open?

How many employees have held the position in the past five years?

Why are the former employees no longer in the position?

What does the company consider the five most important duties of the position to be?

What do you expect the employee you hire to accomplish?

Jot some keywords and concepts from these questions and answers into a page of a small notebook.

WE GO INTO GREATER DETAIL ON QUESTIONS YOU COULD/SHOULD ASK your interviewer in an upcoming chapter.

~

IN OUR NEXT CHAPTER, WE WILL PREPARE TO USE SOME TACTICS THAT will turn the interview in your favour.

7. JOB INTERVIEW DOS

I n this chapter, we will look at a job interview checklist that aims at helping you with turning the job interview to your *advantage*.

JOB INTERVIEW CHECKLIST

Interview "Dos"

SCHEDULE FOR SUCCESS: QUITE OFTEN YOU ARE PROVIDED WITH A TIME for your interview. The interviewers have scheduled it for their convenience that is to fit into their schedule.

If it works for you *good,* go for it. Just make sure you leave enough time for you to travel to the interview allowing time for any problems or obstacles that arise.

AVOID MEAL INTERVIEWS: MEAL INTERVIEWS TEND TO BE AWKWARD affairs. You need to be on your best behavior if you must have one. You are likely being *judged* on your social behavior as much as your job skills.

It is also difficult to answer questions at the same time as you are trying to eat your meal. A busy restaurant can make it very difficult to participate in an interview.

Having said all that ... there are some business owners who want to 'break bread' with a potential job applicant, so they can see what they are like in an informal setting.

ARRIVE ALONE AND ON TIME. DON'T ARRIVE EARLY. ACCLIMATE TO **your environment.** A job interview isn't the time to bring your mother, father or significant other.

You are the one being interviewed, not them!

Plan to arrive at the interview meeting's location no more than 5 to 10 minutes before your meeting is scheduled. It could be awkward for you if the interviewers have scheduled their interviews to close together and you find yourself sitting beside another applicant.

Acclimating to your environment means getting comfortable before you get called in for the interview. If you are wearing a coat and/or a hat, remove them. Be ready to start your interview as soon as you are invited in.

Remember the concept of *first impressions*.

CARRY AN ATTACHÉ CASE. THE TIME OF THE ATTACHÉ CASE HAS LIKELY come and gone unless you are a secret agent or a financial courier where you will likely be handcuffed to one.

Nowadays, there are inexpensive, small soft-shelled file/notebook computer bags that work quite well for carrying a notebook, pens and whatever else you might need for your interview.

ELIMINATE FEAR OF THE UNKNOWN. THIS TAKES SOME WORK ON YOUR part. You should research the company you are applying for work at so you won't be caught off guard with a question about their company.

The old saying of 'knowledge is power' comes into play here. The more you know about the company **the better**.

Talking to current or former employees can be helpful to learn what type of interview questions might be asked.

MAKE THE FIRST IMPRESSION THE BEST. THIS IS THE TIME TO MUSTER UP your courage and project a sense of power, self-control and self-confidence. As we have said before, dress for success.

Make this first impression a *memorable* one, in the right way of course!

GREET THE INTERVIEWER PROPERLY. WHEN MEETING SOMEBODY FOR the first time, the *expectation* is to shake their hand. If the interviewer doesn't offer their hand first, *go for it!* Offer yours!

It might help that *positive* first impression you are aiming at.

Depending on the time of day a greeting such as 'Good morning ...'

'Good afternoon' followed by something to the effect of 'I'm pleased to meet you' is acceptable.'

HONE YOUR HANDSHAKE. WE TALK ABOUT HANDSHAKES IN AN upcoming chapter. You can locate **Whole Lotta Shaking Going On** in the **Additional Resources** section of this book. Hopefully you have been practicing and are comfortable shaking someone's hand.

AVOID ASSUMING A SUBORDINATE ROLE. BY SOME PEOPLE'S ESTIMATION, you *are* in a subordinate role.

They have the *job*, you *want* the job. They have the *power*, you *don't* have the power. That likely works for them, it's their rules. It's time to change the rules, in your favour. You wouldn't have been invited in for the interview if they hadn't thought you were a *worthy* applicant.

That *gives* you power. They have a *problem* to solve. They need to hire somebody who will make them look good. You are a possible *solution*. More *power* for you.

While you are being interviewed and asked questions, if you are able to, use a part of your mind to take a look at what is happening in the interview. Monitor yourself.

Ask yourself if you are being passive or actively engaged in the questions?

In the next chapter, we look at Interviewer personalities. Some will *want* you to be subordinate to them, others *won't* appreciate it.

HAVE YOUR SCRIPT WELL-REHEARSED. WHEN YOU THINK OF A SCRIPT you might be thinking about an actor's lines for a play they are in. In this case, your script would be your answers you have practiced in advance for questions you expect to answer.

. . .

ATTEMPT TO SIT NEXT TO OR NEAR THE INTERVIEWER. GIVEN A CHOICE of seating, it is probably better to sit nearer to your Interviewer rather than further.

Hopefully, the Interviewer isn't sitting behind a big desk, serving as a tool to make them feel important. Some interviews are held at a table. Sitting across from your Interviewer would be better than sitting beside them.

TAKE NOTES.

The idea here is to take some notes to jog your memory after the interview. The challenge of course is to have your note recording, not take away from your being asked questions and you answering them.

It could work against you if the Interviewer believes you are easily distractible.

HAVE AN EXTRA COPY OF YOUR RESUME WITH YOU IN CASE THE **Interviewer doesn't have it.**

It can also come in handy if you need to refer to it to answer an interview question.

EDUCATIONAL BACKGROUND QUESTIONS: SHOW WHAT YOU KNOW! EACH of us has different educational backgrounds. Make use of yours in answering your interview questions. *Show* them you *know you know.*

CHARACTER QUESTIONS: BE CAREFUL! WE DISCUSS THESE AT LENGTH IN an upcoming section.

You will want to answer these types of questions carefully so you look good.

INITIATIVE AND CREATIVITY QUESTIONS: FOCUS ON WHAT AND WHY. I'm reminded of an interview question used by an HR colleague of mine who used to work in the aeronautical field. "How many ping pong balls does it take to fill a 747?

How could anybody possibly know the answer? But a close one would be "I suppose it would depend if you took the seats out or not."

The business she worked for was refitting used 747 airliners and turning them into mail delivery planes. So, the comment about taking the seats out to fit in more, was a valid one.

In this case the HR Manager was looking for *creative thinking* and to see if a *thought-provoking* challenge caused any problems for the applicant.

This would be an example of a thinking *out of the box* answer we hear about so often.

There was no right or wrong answer.

CAREER AND OBJECTIVE QUESTIONS: MAKE IT CLEAR WHAT THEY HEAR. Since the *career and objective statements* have been dropped from usage on our resumes, in favour of *positioning statements*, we need to make it clear to our interviewers, what our plans are.

In an upcoming chapter, we will discuss *career* and *objective* questions. You might hear them in the form of "where do you see yourself in five years?"

ADMIRE SOMETHING IN THE INTERVIEWER'S OFFICE. YOU CAN USE THIS technique to bond with your interviewer. You have to be genuine in doing so though.

If you see something that resonates with you, go for it. If you don't, don't force it. You will come across as phony and it will take away from your interview.

ASSESS THE INTERVIEWER'S STYLE. IN THE NEXT SECTION, WE LOOK AT four different styles of Interviewer's personalities. They aren't the only four and what we talk about may not always hold true, but it does help you in advance to be prepared for whatever you encounter.

"MIRROR" THE INTERVIEWER'S BODY LANGUAGE, FACIAL EXPRESSIONS, **eye movement, rate of speech, tone of voice and rate of breathing.** This is a good technique to master whether you use it in your interview or interactions with other people. It will only work when dealing with an individual, not a group.

The idea behind the technique is if you use the same or similar style of communication as the other person does, they in turn will feel you are resonating with them. As the saying goes, they feel you are on the same wave length.

As mental health therapist, I have good response using the technique when interacting with people who would likely otherwise be hostile to me. The challenge is you don't want to come across as being patronizing or condescending as it will work against you.

ALIGN WITH THE INTERVIEWER. A JOB INTERVIEW *ISN'T* THE PLACE TO get into a philosophical argument with your Interviewer. *Agreeing* with their perspective, assuming you do, can help position you in their mind higher than someone who disagrees with them or is argumentative.

. . .

USE "INSIDER" LANGUAGE. IF YOU ARE APPLYING FOR A POSITION, YOU have previously worked in, you likely have gathered a lot of insider language you can use in your answers. If you haven't worked in the specific field you are applying for, you can help yourself by doing on-line research on the industry.

Using *insider language* helps position you as an *experienced* applicant or at least *knowledgeable* about the field you are applying. You want to be able to score every point you possibly can in your interview. Insider language can help to do so.

FIND AN AREA OF AGREEMENT AND LEAD SLOWLY AND CAREFULLY TO **the offer.** When you are being asked questions by the Interviewer, this may be difficult to do as you are on the defence.

When it comes to *your* turn to ask questions it might be a little easier. The areas of agreement hopefully would be you are the *suitable candidate* for the job vacancy. If you are able to pull it off, they may offer you the job on the spot, pending their following up with checking your references.

BE HONEST, NOT MODEST. IF YOU DONE IT, IT AIN'T BRAGGING. GIVE yourself credit for what you have done and use that experience for *leverage* to solve the employer's problem.

SAY POSITIVE THINGS ABOUT YOUR PRESENT (FORMER) EMPLOYER. YOU can almost guarantee your Interviewer will be on high alert for anything you say about your former or current employer. The belief is if you are eager to bad-mouth them, you would likely do so with your new employer and certainly wouldn't make you a good hire.

. . .

ADMIRE THE ACHIEVEMENTS OF THE PROSPECTIVE EMPLOYER. THIS IS where your pre-interview research can come in handy. If you come up with a gem, fit it in at the appropriate time. Just be sure you come across as being genuine.

BE OBSERVANT. IN ANY DISCUSSION, THERE CAN BE MULTIPLE LEVELS taking place. You might not know what is going on behind the scene, but perhaps the Interviewer might drop hints you should be attuned to. It's kind of like using insider knowledge to your advantage.

REVIEW YOUR NOTES. THIS WOULD BE AFTER THE INTERVIEW OF COURSE.

LIMIT INTERVIEW TO TWO HOURS. HMMM, WHILE IT IS SUGGESTED HERE, I'm not so sure how much control you have over the timing. Perhaps a more complex or demanding job may require a longer interview meeting but it is often divided up into several meetings with different people doing the interviewing.

AT THE END OF THE INTERVIEW THANK THEM FOR THEIR TIME, SHAKE **hands again, and tell them you hope to hear from them soon.** Politeness and manners go a long way in life. Ending the interview and leaving on a *positive note* may make the difference in hiring you or not, it they are undecided.

AS WE SAID EARLIER ABOUT NOT GETTING A *SECOND* CHANCE ABOUT A *first* impression, in this case we are getting a second chance to make an impression. Make it count!

. . .

THESE ARE ALL FACTORS TO TAKE INTO CONSIDERATION TO HELP YOU become the *successful* job applicant.

Of course, you still need to wow them with your interview question answers.

∾

IN THE NEXT CHAPTER, WE EXPLORE SOME THINGS YOU REALLY *DON'T want to do* during your job interview.

8. JOB INTERVIEW DON'TS

We just looked at some strategies we *should* do in preparation and during the interview. Now let's look at some interview Don'ts.

Interview "Don'ts"

DON'T WEAR A COAT, HAT, OR OTHER OUTDOOR CLOTHING INTO THE **interview.** There is usually an outer office area where you can remove your outdoor clothing *prior* to going into the interview room.

Taking off your outdoor clothing once invited into the interview room would likely be awkward but it also takes away those vital first few minutes you have to make a good first impression.

. . .

DON'T WAIT MORE THAN HALF AN HOUR FOR THE INTERVIEWER. WHILE this might be proactive advice, I would say it depends on the situation. If I were told the Interviewer is delayed by unavoidable circumstances, but *really wants* to interview me, I would likely stay.

If I was under the impression, it *didn't seem* there was much priority in the interviewer showing up in time, I might hit the road. I would advise the receptionist or administrative assistant to reschedule the interview if I did decide to leave.

The reality of this situation is it depends on how much personal power you have. If you truly believe you are in a power situation, it may be worth your while to leave.

If you aren't in a position of power and really, really need the job, you might want to be a little more tolerant and stick around for a while.

DON'T ADDRESS THE INTERVIEWER BY HIS OR HER FIRST NAME. AT least, not at first.

If they offer and invite you to call them by their first name, feel free to do so.

Otherwise, stick with a formal address Mr. or Ms. ___ whatever their surname is.

DON'T USE TRITE PHRASES AND/OR TIRED CLICHÉS. MANY PHRASES tend to be tied into the area of the country you live in.

A tired cliché is a saying that may have had some meaning in the past, but has lost its meaning and has become meaningless words.

Some that come to mind are:

... and Bob's your uncle.

... you know what I mean...

... and so on and so forth...

I'm sure you can think of some you have heard many times. The word **Like** has taken on a life of its own for at least one generation.

DON'T SMOKE. I'M SURE IN THE SO-CALLED OLDEN DAYS, THE Interviewer might even offer you a smoke, but those days are long gone.

If you do smoke, try not to smoke before coming in for the interview. A non-smoker can easily smell if you have and you may have blown the interview even before you have started.

DON'T CHEW GUM. SHORT VERSION ... IT IS CONSIDERED BEING unprofessional.

DON'T INTERRUPT. THERE IS AN OLD JOKE THAT GOES... THE BOSS'S Rules: Rule One, the Boss is always right. Rule Two... see Rule One.

It's the Interviewer's show. Like the boss, you need to *let* them think they are right. That doesn't mean you can't correct them if they are wrong, just don't cut them off when they are speaking. They will probably consider you to be rude and will work against you.

DON'T OBJECT TO DISCRIMINATORY QUESTIONS.

In an upcoming section, we look at questions that may be discriminatory in nature.

There may be proactive ways to answer the question without strongly objecting. Just because there may be laws to prevent discriminatory questions, doesn't mean it won't happen.

If you are of a particular group that may face discrimination and you actually do encounter it in a job interview, you may want to give some thought whether you really want to work for this organization.

You have to wonder, if they are discriminatory in a job interview, what would the working conditions be like on a regular basis? You may change your mind about wanting to work for them.

DON'T LOOK AT YOUR WATCH. I HAVEN'T WORN A WATCH IN YEARS SINCE smart phones came out. I can't recall when I have seen anybody else wearing a watch lately.

If you happen to be a person that does wear a watch, looking at it during your interview can work against you. It looks like you have a time commitment to be somewhere else and are not present in the moment.

DON'T READ ANY DOCUMENTS ON THE INTERVIEWER'S DESK. THIS would seem to be one of those common-sense type suggestions, but as the saying goes "common sense isn't so common."

Unless invited to read documents on the Interviewer's desk ... don't!

It looks like there are a lot less things you *shouldn't* be doing than what you *should* be doing.

~

IN THE NEXT SECTION WE LOOK AT **FOUR BASIC INTERVIEWER Personality Types** and offer strategies to levelling the playing field.

SECTION TWO - FOUR BASIC INTERVIEWER PERSONALITY TYPES: OVERVIEW

In this section, we look at how to recognize Four Basic Personality Types you might encounter in a job interview.

There are likely several models out there, but this one seems to work well.

9. TYPE 1 ARE OUTGOING AND DIRECT

T hese people are called 'socializers.' They are energetic, friendly, and self assured.

To spot this personality, look for the following characteristics:

1. A flamboyant style of dress. Even in a conservative business suit, a brightly colored tie, scarf, or jewelry might be worn. Current fashion is preferred to classic styles.

2. They likely have many pictures and personal mementos in the office.

3. They will have a cluttered desk, or at least a covered one.

4. They aren't very time conscious, so you might be kept waiting. In most cases, the Interviewer is juggling a hundred things at once. These types gravitate toward personnel jobs because they're outgoing "people" people.

If you're a methodical, reserved type, you can get into trouble with Interviewers of this type. You'll have to smile, talk faster, and get to the point.

They have to like you before they'll listen to you. And listening isn't on their list.

If you're this type, be careful. You don't want to out talk, out smile or out interview the Interviewer!

∽

IN THE NEXT CHAPTER, WE LOOK AT THE SECOND INTERVIEWER personality type.

10. TYPE 2 ARE SELF CONTAINED AND DIRECT

T his type is referred to as the 'director.' 'Dictator' is more descriptive, though.

These people differ from socializers because they're far more reserved and conservative.

Before unconventional computer kids started running companies, it was believed you had to be like this to make top management. They're still among the high achievers in every field.

Clues to this personality are:

1. They have a conservative, high quality, custom tailored wardrobe, impeccably worn.

2. They have a neat, organized work space. A few expensive personal desk accessories.

Perhaps one or two classic picture frames containing family photos. Nothing flashy. Everything is understated.

3. They have a firm handshake, but not much of a smile. Not as talkative as the first type. They'll size you up critically and wait for you to make your mistakes.

4. Time conscious and annoyed when others are not. They are Goal and bottom line oriented. They Believe all work and no play is the way to spend the day.

To get along with this type, be all business. Don't waste the Interviewer's time. Eliminate unnecessary words and be sincere.

This type itches around 'touchy feely' people. You won't find them saying, "Oh I just adore this." You shouldn't either.

Don't be intimidated, either. If you are, Director types will sense it and reject you immediately. Don't be defensive about weaknesses in your background. Just explain them by turning them into strengths.

∾

IN THE NEXT CHAPTER, WE LOOK AT THE THIRD INTERVIEWER personality type.

11. TYPE 3 ARE SELF CONTAINED
AND INDIRECT

S uch people are called 'thinkers' and might be found in analytical professions. They don't speak up, socialize, or editorialize. They go about their work quietly, and they get it done properly.

Evidence of this personality includes:

1. Uninteresting, understated clothes. Gray and beige predominate. Style and looks aren't a priority, function is. The person is nothing if not practical.

2. They have few personal items and 'warm fuzzies.'

3. This Interviewer's hand will probably dangle at the end of their wrist. Shake it anyway. It will confirm your suspicions he or she is a 'thinker.'

4. They are time conscious and work oriented. Their work ethic is just a strong as the Directors', but Thinkers don't want to run things, they are loners.

5. They will probably have an organized desk, with neatly arranged work. Maybe even a 'to do' list with half the items crossed off.

This type of person is hard to draw out and may become annoyed if you try. If you're pushy and aggressive, the thinker gets withdrawn and your offer will be withheld.

Answer questions directly and succinctly. Volunteer as much information as the Interviewer needs to make a decision. Thinkers thrive on data, but they need time to analyze it, so don't rush.

~

IN THE NEXT CHAPTER, WE LOOK AT THE FOURTH INTERVIEWER personality type.

YOUR VISION OF YOURSELF AND YOUR POSSIBILITIES IS A MENTAL picture of what you will become. We must carve our own success in the same way that a sculptor chips away at a block of marble. Like the sculptor who creates a masterpiece from a mental model, we must begin our journey to success by visualizing what we want to become. The trouble with most people is that they never dare to realize their highest possibilities. They misuse their imagination by daydreaming and wishing their lives away. Think positive and clearly visualize your possibilities. Positive visualizations will help you seize the opportunity for greatness within you. --- Anon

12. TYPE 4 ARE OUTGOING AND INDIRECT

The most common word for this personality type is 'helper.' They're friendly, like socializers, but without the aggressiveness.

Helpers tend to gravitate toward 'human resources'; they're the closest the business world gets to providing psychiatric social work for employees. Helpers take time to know you before the actual interview begins.

They're nice, but will do almost anything to avoid making a decision. In area, you need to help them.

You're probably talking to a helper when there is:

I. A nonthreatening appearance that matches their demeanour. They wear natural shades and soft fabrics.

2. They have a number of personal items on the desk, often hand-made. Their office will reflect other people are important to them.

3. They have a friendly, expressive, and concerned approach. Helpers may apologize for keeping you waiting because they were busy solving everyone else's problems.

They smile warmly, reach out to take your hand, and might never let it go.

4. They will probably have a phone ringing, work piling up, and many uncompleted projects. To a helper, 'people' are all that matters.

These people are the opposite of the 'director' type, and they rarely play opposite each other.

The helper never gives up trying to convince the director to "human-ize," "personalize," and "realize".

To get hired, take time to establish rapport, become friends, and accentuate the importance of the 'person' in 'personnel.' But remember to limit interviews to two hours.

With helpers, it's your responsibility to get your job qualifications across. If you don't, you may leave the interview with a friend but not a job.

They won't ask you to give them a reason to hire you or even recom-mend you for a second interview. Emotionally, they don't realize that's why you're there. They think it's because you're taking a hiring survey. A helper helps, but doesn't hire.

THIS IS A REMARKABLY ACCURATE WAY TO OUT STEREOTYPE THE stereotypers. Some will fit the description exactly, others will fit several.

No matter. Just know and play to your audience. Study the four profiles and practice typecasting a few of your friends, coworkers, and relatives.

Learn to pick up on the clues to someone's predominant personality style. Then practice playing to them. They're your audience too.

Picking up clues from a person's appearance, speech, and body language can serve you in many ways throughout your career. In short, while you are concentrating on making a good impression, you also need to be absorbing a clear impression of everybody and everything else.

$$\sim$$

IN THE NEXT SECTION, WE WILL DISCUSS COMMON INTERVIEW QUESTIONS and strategies on how to answer them.

"DEFINE YOUR GOALS IN TERMS OF THE ACTIVITIES NECESSARY TO achieve them, and concentrate on those activities." -- Brian Tracy

"DEVELOP AND MAINTAIN MOMENTUM BY WORKING CONTINUOUSLY toward your sales goals every day." -- Brian Tracy

START BY DOING WHAT'S NECESSARY; THEN DO WHAT'S POSSIBLE; AND suddenly you are doing the impossible. -- St. Francis of Assisi

SECTION THREE: INTERVIEW QUESTIONS

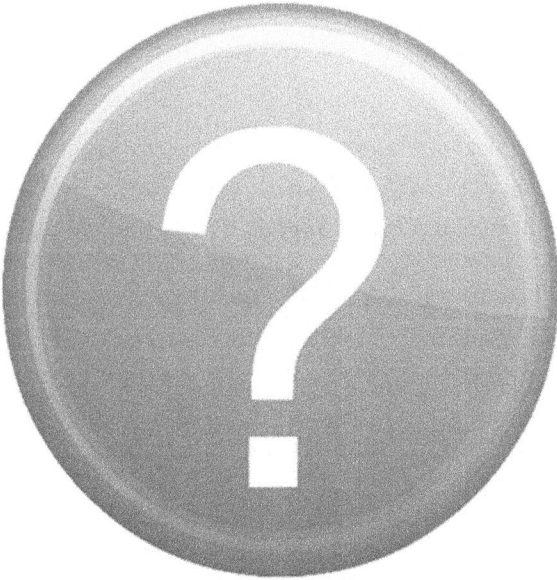

13. COMMON INTERVIEW QUESTIONS

O verview

IF YOU ARE APPLYING FOR A JOB, ANY JOB, YOU CAN EXPECT YOU WILL BE asked to participate in an interview. It could be face-to-face or could be over the phone, internet or Skype.

THERE ARE LIKELY COUNTLESS QUESTIONS YOU COULD BE ASKED AND some you *shouldn't* be asked due to equal rights legislation, etc.

Many employers have developed their own questions related to their specific field of business.

By practicing your responses to some of these questions, hopefully you will not be taken off guard if asked one of them.

Yes, there are lots of them provided here.

One of the best ways to deal with these questions, is to give some thought to how you would answer each of them. You will note the questions have been organized into categories to help you focus and some of them seem to the same question, asked in different ways. They are!

You need to be able to think about each question your Interviewer asks you.

What are they *really* asking you?

You may want to review **Chapter 5 Organizing Your Presentation** where we explored several methods of answering questions in general, but specifically interview questions.

If you are momentarily stumped by a question, don't panic. Ask the Interviewer if you could come back to the question later.

If the question truly does stump you, hopefully you will be able to think of a response while you are answering other questions.

I once went for a job interview and was peppered with 42 separate questions for over an hour and a half. My wife wasn't too thrilled as it was mid-February in Canada, and she was sitting in the car waiting for me, freezing.

When you are practicing your responses, you should have somebody help you by asking you questions randomly from the list.

There can be a significant difference in how you answer a question *in your mind* and how you say it orally. Practice saying your answers out loud.

It can be helpful to record yourself on a recording device such as a smart phone for the audio or a camera that records video. You can then play back the question and response to determine if you might have handled it differently.

Most importantly, relax, go with the flow, and before you know it, you'll be in your next job.

I have broken the content of this section into categories of questions to try to keep it manageable.

Each category of questions will have its own chapter for simplicity.

Note: Indicates some background information or industry advice has been provided for you to consider.

~

"WATCH YOUR THOUGHTS, THEY BECOME WORDS;

watch your words, they become actions;

watch your actions, they become habits;

watch your habits, they become character;

watch your character, for it becomes your destiny."

— Frank Outlaw

14. INTERVIEW QUESTIONS TO ASSESS YOUR EDUCATION

- **How does your experience and education qualify you for this job?**

S elect four to five accomplishments or skills based on what you have learned from the job description and the information you provided on your resumé.

- **How does your education qualify you for this job?**

This is basically the same question as the last one except focusing on your *education*, excluding your experience.

As the question asks, you should stay focused on your education that is *relevant* to the position you are applying for.

- **Why did you choose to attend the college you are attending?**

This assumes of course you are still in school. Be prepared for a follow-up question about your availability if you are still in school.

- What aspect of your education applies to this position?

This is another version of how does your education qualify you for this job?

1. What training have you received that qualifies you for this job?

Training is a little different from your *education*. It usually involves a shorter course period and the 'training' content tends to be hands on.

You can include any *live* training, where you were *physically* present in the room with the trainer, or any on-line training you have taken such as with this course.

The idea remains that you need to be focused on the particular job you are applying for.

- What have you done outside of formal education to improve yourself?

This would be a place to mention your training courses you have taken as in the previous question.

- What training opportunities have you taken advantage of and why?

This question adds a bit of a twist to the training question. It's asking for the courses but it is also asking you to *justify* why you took the courses.

Once again, you need to be focused on what training courses you mention as well as being able to provide your justification for taking them. 'It felt like a good idea at the time' probably wouldn't be a good answer.

- **What additional training will we have to provide for you if we hire you?**

This might be a kind of trick question. If you provide a list of areas you need training in, you might come across as needing too much investment in you to hire you.

If you don't provide any suggestions, they may interpret it as you *not* having a clear understanding of the job they are offering.

One solution may be to say something to the effect that you will require a new-hire orientation to the job.

❧

IN THE NEXT CHAPTER, WE WILL LOOK AT **WORK EXPERIENCE Questions.**

15. WORK EXPERIENCE QUESTIONS

I n this chapter, we look at **Work Experience Questions.** Starting off with...

- **Tell us about yourself.**

FOCUS ON THE ASPECTS OF YOUR *WORK EXPERIENCE* THAT APPLY specifically to the position you're applying.

This can also take the form of, "if I asked one of your faculty members/previous supervisors to tell me about you, what would they say?"

Your answer should spotlight the education, experience, and work ethic that matches what the employer is seeking in an employee. End by saying you are *well prepared* for the position the interviewer is trying to fill.

- **What would you like me to know about you?**

KEEP THE ANSWER *SHORT* AND *POWER-PACKED*. IDENTIFY FOUR TO FIVE qualities that make you a strong candidate.

Highlight your academic achievements, ability to do the type of work you are interviewing for, and your work ethic.

- **How are you qualified for this job?**

I CAN'T LOCATE THE SOURCE OF THIS FACT BUT I HAD READ IF YOU HAVE 75% of the qualifications required for any position, you will likely be eligible, at least for an interview.

This is your time to shine! Your response should be consistent with the info you have featured in your resume.

- **How does your current job qualify you for this position?**

IF YOU ARE APPLYING FOR AN *INTERNAL* JOB, MEANING YOU ALREADY work for the company, this may be easy to answer. The Interviewer may have knowledge of your current job's duties.

If you work elsewhere, you will need to provide solid examples of how it will qualify you. Be prepared for a follow-up question of why are you wanting to leave your current position.

- **How does your experience qualify you for this job?**

WHAT HAVE YOU DONE THAT PREPARES YOU FOR THE RESPONSIBILITIES of this job?

Review what the employer is looking for (job description and any information a recruiter or career service staff member may have given you) and develop examples of how your academic work directly relates to the job responsibilities.

- **Describe a typical day at your present position.**

YOU MAY WANT TO REVIEW YOUR JOB DESCRIPTION FOR YOUR CURRENT position in preparation for this question being asked.

If your current job bores you, you may want to ignore *that* fact and show yourself in an optimistic, enthusiastic manner. Don't make yourself the hero of your story.

- **What were your three greatest accomplishments on your last job?**

WHILE YOU LIKELY HAVE PERSONAL ACCOMPLISHMENTS TO MENTION, YOU would be better off giving examples of accomplishments that benefitted the employer.

You can take credit for the work you did and you should, but it likely puts you in a better light if you show you are willing to go the extra step to achieve an accomplishment that benefits the employer.

- **What are some things on your current job you have done well?**

THESE SHOULD BE FEATURED IN YOUR RESUME, ALLOWING YOU TO PULL them from there.

- **What is the most difficult assignment you have had?**

THIS IS A QUESTION THAT ALLOWS YOU TO HIGHLIGHT YOUR SKILLS, however the Interviewer is likely looking at how you handled success or failure.

What did you learn from the assignment? What would you do differently?

- **What accomplishment on the job are you the most proud of?**

ONCE AGAIN, YOU SHOULD PROBABLY USE AN EXAMPLE THAT BENEFITED the Employer in some way. You want to be seen as a team player, not a soloist.

- **What steps have you taken to improve your job skills?**

YOU COULD FOCUS ON YOUR CONTINUING EDUCATIONAL TRAINING AS evidenced in the educational segment of your resume, assuming you have of course.

- **What significant contributions have you made to the operation of your work group?**

THIS QUESTION SETS YOU UP TO SHOW YOURSELF AS A TEAM PLAYER.

- **How has your current position prepared you to take on greater responsibilities?**

MAYBE YOUR CURRENT JOB HAS, OR MAYBE IT HASN'T. AS YOU GO forward to interviewing for a new job, give some consideration to your current job.

What have been its advantages? What skills did you develop while in this job?

This should lead you to developing an answer relating to increased responsibility.

- **What makes you more qualified than the other candidates?**

THIS ISN'T THE TIME TO BE FLIPPANT AND RESPOND WITH "I'M SMARTER ... better looking ... desperate etc."

This is a difficult question to answer as you have no way of knowing the qualifications of the other candidates. The only real response you have available to you is to reinforce the qualifications and experience you have to bring to the job.

- **Why do you want to leave your current job?**

THIS IS A QUESTION TO BE CAUTIOUS OF. YOU NEED TO KEEP YOUR response positive in nature.

If your reason for leaving is due to interpersonal conflict with co-workers or supervisors, you need to avoid commenting on it. If you do, the Interviewer may jump to the conclusion you will likely do the same for them.

That doesn't make you a desirable hire.

THE FOLLOWING TWO QUESTIONS ARE VERSIONS OF ONES WE LOOKED AT earlier.

- **How has your job prepared you to take on greater responsibility?**

- **Tell us about your qualifications for this position.**

THE NEXT TWO QUESTIONS FOCUS ON YOUR EXPERIENCE AGAIN:

- **What actions have you taken in the past 10 years to prepare you for this position?**

- **What steps have you taken in the past two years to improve your qualifications?**

HOWEVER, THIS TIME THEY ARE LOOKING FOR WHAT *ACTIONS OR STEPS* you have taken.

Once again, you can refer to the *Experience* section of your resume and come up with a comment you are comfortable saying to the effect you believe in continually challenging yourself and building your skills.

- **In the areas where your experience falls short for this job, what steps will you take to make up for this shortfall?**

THIS QUESTION IS SIMILAR TO AN EARLIER ONE THAT ASKED WHAT training are we going to have to provide you if we hire you?

The *difference* with this question is they are looking for *you* to *analyze* your skill sets to see if you have shortcomings and how *you*, not them, are going to solve it.

- **Describe yourself.**

THIS WOULD BE A GOOD PLACE TO DELIVER AN EXPANDED VERSION OF your Summary Statement.

There is a value in developing your elevator pitch that includes your USP (Universal Sales Pitch) so you could deliver it to respond to this question.

There is a chapter about developing your USP located in the Additional Resources Section of the book.

- **What skills and abilities do you have?**

ONCE AGAIN, REFER TO THE CONTENT OF YOUR RESUME.

You want to reinforce the fact you have the skills to take on the job and you want to come across from a position of strength.

- **Recall an incident where you made a major mistake. What did you do after the mistake was made? What did you learn from this mistake?**

THIS CAN BE CHALLENGING TO ANSWER IN IT STARTS OFF WITH HAVING you look bad. Be careful what situation you use to answer this one.

You need one that has a *teachable moment* as its outcome. "Well I certainly won't do that again!" isn't a good response.

The Interviewer is looking to see you are capable of learning from your mistakes.

- **What is the greatest failure you've had? What would you have done differently?**

THIS IS ANOTHER VERSION OF THE PREVIOUS QUESTION.

- **What action on the job are you the least proud of?**

GIVE SOME SERIOUS THOUGHT AS TO HOW YOU WILL ANSWER THIS ONE. It can backfire on you and shed a negative light on you.

You don't want the Interviewer to think that is what your character is like, based on the one example you have given.

One way to answer it may be to provide a response that is fairly benign and then show how you *learned or grew* from the incident.

- **Tell us about a difficult situation that you encountered and how you resolved it.**

THIS QUESTION IS SIMILAR TO OTHERS BUT IS ASKING *HOW* YOU RESOLVED it.

Your problem-solving skills are being assessed in this question. The Interviewer is looking to see if you used any kind of problem-solving process and/or took a leadership position in solving the problem.

- **Where do you see yourself in five years?**

THE EMPLOYER IS ASKING BECAUSE HE OR SHE WANTS TO KNOW IF YOU plan to go to work for one of their competitors after you complete your initial training.

Respond by letting the Interviewer know if you plan to stay in the position for which you are interviewing or to move up in the organization.

~

IN THE NEXT CHAPTER WE LOOK AT QUESTIONS RELATED TO YOUR resume.

16. RESUME RELATED INTERVIEW QUESTIONS

$\mathbf{T}$ his chapter looks at resume-related questions.

- **Take us through your resume.**

THIS IS AN EXAMPLE OF WHY YOU SHOULD HAVE AN EXTRA COPY OF YOUR resume with you when you go for the interview.

Starting off with your Summary Statement, you could read it word for word. Or you could give an expanded elevator pitch style of response.

Then you work your way through your experience that should reflect upon the job description and duties for the job you are applying for.

Continue on with outlining your education that qualifies you for the job.

- **What are you most proud of on your resume?**

This is a question you will have to answer on your own. Pride can get you in trouble and highlight you in a way that you don't want.

You would likely be better in choosing something that shares your pride with others as in your part of being a team member on a specific project or perhaps sharing an accomplishment with others.

∼

In the next chapter, we look at some general interview questions.

"Whatever your talent is, you should craft it, nourish it and build on it. It is the 'niche talent' that will take you to the top of your field." -- Mark Victor Hansen

"Identify and develop your unique talents and abilities, the things that make you special." -- Brian Tracy

17. GENERAL INTERVIEW QUESTIONS

This chapter looks at interview questions I have given the classification of General as they don't seem to fit elsewhere.

- **Tell me a story.**

GEAR YOUR STORIES TO GIVE THE LISTENER A FEELING YOU COULD FIT in... you could do the job here.

- **In what way do you think you can contribute to our company?**

PREPARING TO ANSWER THIS QUESTION REQUIRES A 2-STEP PREPARATION: *assessing* your skills and *researching* the needs of the company.

An integral part of skill assessment (looking at your own experience, education and talents) is to 'skill-match'. Considering the job opening, what are the skills needed?

Make a list of the requisite skills (in priority order) and then list concrete examples of your possession of the skill.

For example: a sales representative would need good interpersonal skills, the ability to deal with difficult people. For 'proof' of this skill, you could list experiences and examples of how you were *successful* in a difficult situation.

These matched skills are your *key selling points*.

Next, what appears to be the current problems at the organization, based upon your research? What are their needs you can meet?

In other words, given the specifics of the company, what value can you add?

After these two steps, you are in a great position to come up with concrete examples of what you can offer the company.

This question, by the way, is just another version of "Why should we hire you?"

In the interview, when asked this question, you could respond with: "In my experience in sales, I know having the ability to deal effectively with all types of people is not merely a positive element --- it is an essential one.

With your plans to expand into ___ market, a sales representative with a proven ability to meet with all types of people and to be able to assess and meet their immediate needs would be a great asset.

In the past _ years, I have increased sales..."

The next few questions refer to your career.

Just to be clear, a *career* refers to different jobs or positions you have taken within a specific field.

As an example, I'm a Registered Nurse and presumably would be looking for other positions within the healthcare field, specifically nursing.

I could very well change my career and go into something completely different from nursing. Many people do so.

I'm just going to go over them quickly as they seem to be fairly straightforward.

- Where do you want to be 5 years from now in your career?
- What are your long-term career goals?
- What prompted you to take your current job?
- Where do you see yourself 10 years from now?
- Why did you make a career change?
- Why do you want to leave your current position?
- Five years ago, where did you see yourself today?
- What is your career goal?

ALL OF THESE QUESTIONS ARE ASKING YOU TO ILLUSTRATE YOU ACTUALLY have given some thought to our career path.

Your answer should show you have. It's not just a matter of job jumping, you need to be able to illustrate you have a lifelong career plan in place.

∽

IN THE NEXT CHAPTER, WE LOOK AT INTERVIEW QUESTIONS THAT ASSESS your analytic skills.

18. QUESTIONS TO ASSESS YOUR ANALYTIC SKILLS

These next questions relate to the Interviewer assessing your analytic skills.

If you are applying for a job that relies on their worker's technical and problem-solving skills, you will need to be prepared for these types of questions.

- Are you analytical? Give us one example of your analytical abilities.
- Tell us about your analytical skills.
- Tell us about a particularly difficult problem that you analyzed and what was your recommendation.
- What steps do you take when analyzing complex problems?
- How would you rate your analytical ability? Why?
- How would your manager rate your analytical ability?

If you have recent performance appraisal results, this would be a good place to use your supervisor's exact words.

- Tell us about a situation where the analysis that you performed was incorrect. What would you have done differently?

THIS IS ANOTHER VERSION OF A QUESTION ASKED EARLIER WHERE YOU were asked to come up with a situation that didn't go well and how you turned it around.

- What do you know about our company?

DO YOU KNOW THE COMPANY'S PRODUCTS/SERVICES, MISSION statement, headquarters location, and name of the CEO?

If not, do a 5-minute internet search on the company.

If you have this information, take the time to look up Interviewer(s) on LinkedIn and notice where they went to school and their history with the company.

(**Hint:** interviewers often like to reflect on their educational experience. Knowing where they went to school can be helpful.)

∾

OUR NEXT CHAPTER FOCUSES ON **COMMUNICATION SKILLS** QUESTIONS.

19. COMMUNICATION SKILLS ASSESSMENT QUESTIONS

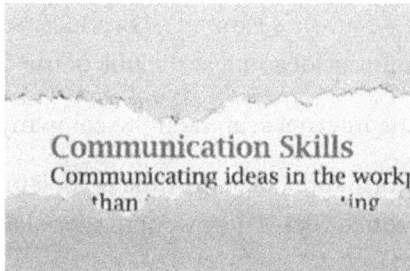

Communication Skills
Communicating ideas in the workp
than   ing

This chapter focuses on questions that help the Interviewer *assess* your *communication* skills.

Communication skills fit into the category of *soft skills* and some may tell you they are every bit as important as your *hard* skills.

After-all, if you aren't able to get along with your co-workers and supervisors, you likely aren't a good hire.

I'm just going to list them and wait to comment at the end.

- **How do you effectively communicate with others?**
- **How important is listening to effective communications?**
- **What are some characteristics of a good listener?**

- Tell us about a situation where you demonstrated good communications skills.
- Tell us about a situation where you demonstrated poor communications skills. What would you have done differently?
- How would you rate your communications skills? Why?

IF YOU HAVE WELL-DEVELOPED COMMUNICATION SKILLS, GOOD FOR YOU.

If not, you may want to spend some time researching the topic and seeing if you can develop some specific skills in advance of your interview.

At the very least, learning some new communication skills will help you understand what the Interviewer is looking for in your responses and help you to develop some answers.

Good communication at every level of an organization is important.

You can pretty well expect there will be at least one question on the subject.

Being prepared for these questions may score you some points and answering them well, may illustrate you do indeed have good communication skills.

It's one thing to say you have them, but answering your questions as efficiently as you can, helps prove the point.

In this next segment, we offer a few questions about communicating with your Co-workers.

- **What are some rules to follow to insure effective communications with your co-workers?**

This question would seem to focus on what you consider to be rules.

Hopefully, the Interviewer will see them the same way as you do.

It would be worth your while to determine if there actually are any rules and what they might be.

Think *respect*. Think *assertive communication*.

- **What are some of the means of communication in the workplace?**

This question appears to be designed to test your understanding of the communication process.

Your answer should include: 1 to 1 conversations, e-mail 1 to 1 discussions, mass e-mails through distribution lists, written memos on paper, they still exist and don't forget the grapevine.

It exists in every work-site and you will want to be tuned into it.

It wouldn't hurt to offer that gossip also exists, which is a little different from the grapevine and it has a negative effect in the workplace in many ways.

And you, of course, don't participate in it!

- **How would your co-workers rate your communications skills?**

YOU MAY WANT TO ASK SOME OF YOUR CO-WORKERS THIS QUESTION. You may not like the answers you get but it would help you to genuinely answer the question.

The secret to answering the question effectively may lay in you sharing what you learned about how your co-workers have commented about your communication skills and what you are doing about it.

IN THE NEXT SEGMENT, WE LOOK AT QUESTIONS RELATED TO communicating with your supervisor.

Communicating with Supervisors:

- **Communicating with your supervisor is an important aspect of all of our jobs. In addition to being brief, what guidelines should you follow to communicate effectively with your supervisor?**

I would expect there isn't a definitive answer to this question but some things come to mind from my experience.

- choose your time. Supervisors can be busy people. Your communication will probably be better received if you speak to them at a time when they are not working on other activities and you have their undivided attention.

- for important discussions have multiple details, I would suggest sending a follow-up e-mail outlining the important points that were discussed.

- clarify the purpose of communicating with your supervisor in advance. Are you informing them of something, are you explaining your role or actions you took in a specific situation, are you asking for their assistance or additional resources, or are you merely updating them, what we call an FYI?

- What are the reasons for communicating upwards to your superiors?

HERE ARE SOME EXAMPLES, BUT ONCE AGAIN, DEVELOP SOME OF our own.

- Sharing information as to your progress or lack of on a specific topic or project. Updating them on any resources you might need to complete your task.
- Advising them of potential risks or the opposite of sharing with them something that went really well.

- How would your supervisor rate your communications skills?

THEY'RE LIKELY LOOKING FOR SOMETHING MORE THAN A "GOOD!" AS AN answer to this question.

If your communication skills are good and you have evidence from a performance appraisal validating a supervisor has said that they are good, you may want to prepare to paraphrase what was said to your benefit.

If your communication skills *aren't* up to snuff and it has been recognized by a supervisor that they need improvement, you can likely turn this to your favour by *admitting* that they aren't as good as they should be *however*, you are *actively* working on steps to improve them.

- How do you like to be managed/ supervised?

THE EMPLOYER IS REALLY ASKING *HOW MUCH* SUPERVISION YOU NEED. BE honest, but understand employers select candidates who *know* when to ask questions and *when* to work independently.

This next segment offers some suggestions for questions that may be asked if you are applying for a supervisory position.

If you are not applying for a supervisory position, you may want to move forward in the program to the next segment.

These following questions are testing your knowledge of the supervisory process.

If you have supervisory experience to draw from, you will want to provide some answers based on your experience.

- **How can a supervisor establish effective communications with staff?**

SOME SUPERVISORS FEEL AN OPEN-DOOR POLICY IS BEST. THIS IS WHERE the employees are told that your door is open all the time and they should feel free to come to you to talk about their problems.

The downside, for supervisors who have a tendency to micromanage, is it can create a culture where the employees get used to running to the boss to solve all problems.

It can also create a situation where individual employees are competing for attention from the supervisor and use dysfunctional interpersonal communication techniques to meet their needs.

On, the other hand, an open-door policy can foster good communications with your workers if you set up your expectations in the first place.

Some examples might be... if you have a problem with a co-worker, talk to them first to try to resolve the issue. If you are unable to resolve it, then come to me.

You could encourage a 'no-gossip' policy. If you are coming to complain about another and you haven't tried to resolve it, well then go back to them and try.

Don't accept unilateral complaining from employees about other employees.

- **What means of communication may be used to effectively establish a new policy?**

Over my career, I have been involved in all aspects of policy and procedures.

When I was in my younger rebel years, I found many policies & procedures were created to control me or stop me from doing something I shouldn't have been doing.

The simplest way to establish a new policy in the workplace is to post it to a Policy & Procedure Manual with the expectation all employees will read it.

Simple yes, effective no.

In most cases, it would be more effective to discuss the new policy with those it effects at a staff meeting.

Employees need to know the importance of the policy, assuming there really is importance.

Everyone needs to know the policy exists and the purpose it was designed for.

- **Are there additional considerations in communicating to groups of employees versus individual employees?**

A WISE RULE OF THUMB IS TO *PRAISE* IN PUBLIC AND TO *CRITICIZE* IN private.

Too bad many supervisors don't know about it or choose not to.

- **What are some good rules to keep in mind when directing employees?**

HERE ARE SOME EXAMPLES. YOU SHOULD BE PREPARED TO SUPPLY your own.

- Your expectations should be clearly outlined.
- What is the desired end result of the employee completing a task?
- Are you delegating any responsibility or authority to the specific employee?
- Are there any time constraints involved?
- That is, are you expecting partial or complete results by a certain time?

- **In what instances, is written communication better than verbal communications?**

IN AN EMPLOYEE CONTRACT OR WORK AGREEMENT, THE TERMS OF employment would be helpful.

Another example relates to employee performance standards, where a Letter of Expectation might be issued to the employee from the Employer, outlining performance expectations have not been met and the consequences should the expectations not be met by a certain date.

Yet another example would be the organization's policy and procedure manual that specifically outlines situations and actions the employee would need as a reference rather than going by memory of an oral conversation

~

IN THE NEXT CHAPTER, WE LOOK AT DECISION MAKING QUESTIONS.

20. DECISION-MAKING PROCESS QUESTIONS

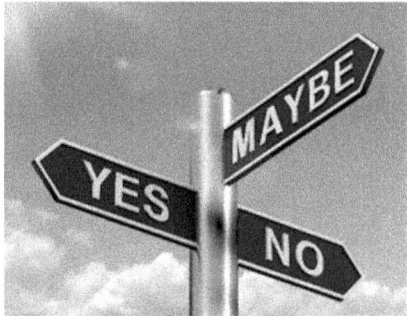

T his chapter looks at questions that assess your *decision-making* processes.

- **What type of decisions do you make in your current position?**

EVERY POSITION HAS ELEMENTS OF IT THAT REQUIRE YOU TO MAKE decisions whether they be minor ones or those that have a greater impact.

Choose some examples where your decisions have had a positive response and focus you in a favourable light.

- **What decisions are easiest for you to make and which ones are the most difficult? Why?**

IN ADDRESSING THE DECISIONS THAT ARE THE MOST DIFFICULT FOR YOU, don't cite decisions that are essential to the job you are interviewing for.

For the decisions that you do cite, expand your answer by telling what steps you're taking to improve your decision making.

- **What steps are involved in making a decision?**

THIS QUESTION MAY BE A LITTLE MORE COMPLICATED THAN IT SEEMS. The interviewer is testing your decision-making processes.

You may want to do some research on this topic to be prepared.

Something to think about is many decisions are based on one's logical thoughts vs their emotional ones. In sales, many purchases are made on emotion, but justified by logic.

Many people use a pro vs con approach. What happens if I take this approach, what happens if I don't.

- **What items of information do *you* typically need before you make a decision?**

REMEMBER, THERE ARE NO PERFECT DECISIONS AND IN MANY situations, you will never have all the facts.

This question seems to be asking about your decision-making process so you will need to provide specifics, rather than generalities.

- **Give us an example of your ability to make decisions under pressure.**

ONCE AGAIN, YOU ARE BEING ASSESSED. SO, PROVIDE AN EXAMPLE OR two with favourable results and that make you look good.

- **Tell us about the worst decision that you've made on the job.**

BE CAREFUL WITH THIS ONE!

You want to make it look like you are capable of learning from bad decisions and not that you regularly make bad decisions.

- **Tell us about the best decision that you've made on the job.**

HERE IS ANOTHER OPPORTUNITY FOR SHINING.

- **How would you rate a job that requires you to constantly make decisions?**

I'M NOT REALLY SURE WHAT IS BEING ASKED HERE.

I would suspect they are really asking "how would you do working in our job that requires you to constantly make decisions?"

~

OUR NEXT CHAPTER LOOKS AT WHAT WOULD OTHERS SAY ABOUT YOU.

(1) YOU CLEARLY DECIDE WHAT IT IS THAT YOU'RE ABSOLUTELY **committed to achieving,**

(2) YOU'RE WILLING TO TAKE MASSIVE ACTION,

(3) YOU NOTICE WHAT'S WORKING OR NOT, AND

(4) **You continue to change your approach until you achieve what you want, using whatever life gives you along the way.**

— ANTHONY ROBBINS, 1960-, AMERICAN AUTHOR, SPEAKER, PEAK Performance Expert/ Consultant

"PEOPLE WHO ARE UNABLE TO MOTIVATE THEMSELVES MUST BE CONTENT **with mediocrity, no matter how impressive their other talents."** — Andrew Carnegie

"WHEN YOU KNOW WHAT YOU WANT, AND YOU WANT IT BAD ENOUGH, you will find a way to get it." — Jim Rohn

21. WHAT WOULD OTHERS SAY ABOUT YOU INTERVIEW QUESTIONS

This chapter addresses what you expect different people would say about you if they were asked. In this area of questioning you are likely better to appear *humble*, yet *self-confident*.

These following three questions can likely be answered well by referring to any recent performance appraisals.

That way you are using your supervisor's own words for your answer.

- **What do you think your supervisor would say about your work?**

- What do you think your co-worker would say about your work?
- What would your boss say about you - both positive and negative?
- What would your subordinates say about - both positive and negative?

THIS QUESTION PRESUMES YOU HAVE OTHER EMPLOYEES AND YOU oversee various aspects of their job performance.

This can be a challenging question to answer in that most of the time, we don't ask our subordinates what they think of us. Perhaps we are probably better off not knowing.

- What would your co-workers say about you - both positive and negative?

IT CAN BE EASY TO RESPOND TO THE POSITIVE THOUGHTS OUR CO-workers think but not so the negative.

Unless you are a mind-reader, this question can be difficult to answer. You may get by with acknowledging you aren't a mind-reader but then provide some examples of how you sense people respond to you.

It is a fact not everybody in the world will get along with you, so if you do have some you don't get along with, it *won't* necessarily work against you.

- What three keywords would your peers use to describe you?

THIS IS A CHALLENGING QUESTION. IF YOU DON'T KNOW, GO AHEAD AND ask them.

You will probably get different answers from everyone, so see if there are any themes that come up consider them and choose three of them.

- **What one thing would your boss say that he or she has the greatest problem with you?**

HOPEFULLY, YOU WILL NEVER BE ASKED THIS QUESTION.

Choose something benign.

I once had a manager say in a performance appraisal the only negative thing she had to say about me was she wished she had more time to spend with me.

I've always taken is as she enjoyed her time with me.

Now I think about it... I'm hoping she didn't mean I needed a lot of help from her.

Hmm. No, I don't think so!

- **Describe a situation in which your work was criticized?**

- **Describe the situation and how you responded to the criticism.**

THIS QUESTION REFERS TO YOUR WORK BEING *CRITICIZED* RATHER THAN you receiving *constructive feedback*.

Likely, most people respond to criticism in the way it was delivered to them.

Criticism is *negative* in nature. Some believe *launching* a counter-attack can be a good defence.

In this case a good answer would include you accepting the criticism, accepting it in the sense you *agree* to consider its merit.

Then you would ask the criticizer to back up the points they have made with examples. If generalizations have been made, you could point out the inaccuracies.

A productive way of dealing with unfair criticism includes you taking an *assertive* approach to challenging the individual who has criticized you.

Just *because* they have said something about you, doesn't *necessarily* make it *true*.

If you haven't responded effectively to criticism in the past, you can probably turn it to your advantage in the interview question by *briefly* describing a situation you didn't handle well but explain you have *learned* how to deal with it assertively and will handle it differently in the future.

This could be an example of the Past, Present and Future model for answering a question we talked about a few chapters back.

You are in essence, turning a negative into a positive example that will help make you look better.

- **How would your subordinates describe you?**

THIS IS A DIFFERENT VERSION OF A QUESTION WE LOOKED AT EARLIER.

- **Tell us about the last time you lost your temper?**

- What situations *make* you lose your temper?

IF YOU'RE NOT A PERSON WHO LOSES THEIR TEMPER, SAY SO.

If you *are*, be *careful* with your response.

Losing one's temper is often related to *not having* the skills to solve a particular problem.

The Interviewer is testing your ability to problem solve and remain in control of yourself with the situation you find yourself in.

- Tell us about the worst supervisor you've worked under.

THIS CAN BE A LOADED QUESTION.

You will need to provide examples of why they were the worst and how you were able to work with them or not.

- Tell us about the *best* supervisor you've worked under.

GIVEN THIS QUESTION YOU COULD HIGHLIGHT THE SUPERVISOR'S positive attributes you have liked.

Actions such as they were a good teacher or mentor would be helpful.

- Tell us about a confrontation that you've had with a co-worker.

THE IMPORTANT PART OF RESPONDING TO THIS QUESTION WOULD BE IN sharing how you successfully resolved the confrontation and moved forward in working together.

- **How do you maintain an effective working relationship with your coworkers?**

THIS IS AN INTERESTING QUESTION AS IT IS ASSESSING YOUR WORKING skills.

Getting along with your co-workers is important. Certainly, for you, but perhaps even more for your manager.

They don't want to be spending all their time intervening in employee interpersonal conflict. It takes away from more important work they should be doing.

- **How would your best friend describe you?**

THIS ONE SHOULD BE FAIRLY EASY TO ANSWER. I WOULD EXPECT YOU have many things in common and hopefully your best friend is supportive of you.

If not, maybe it's time to get a new best friend.

- **How would your worst enemy describe you?**

I WOULD SUGGEST STAYING FAIRLY NEUTRAL AND REPLY YOU DON'T believe or are aware you have any enemies, let alone a worst enemy.

Admitting you do could lead you to follow-up questions you wouldn't want to answer and certainly wouldn't make you look good.

~

IN OUR NEXT CHAPTER, WE LOOK AT STRENGTHS VS WEAKNESSES Interview Questions

"SOME MEN HAVE THOUSANDS OF REASONS WHY THEY CANNOT DO WHAT they want to, when all they need is one reason why they can." – Mary Frances Berry, US government official, author. She was chief educational officer of U.S., 1977-80.

"THE BEST MOTIVATION IS SELF-MOTIVATION. THE GUY SAYS, 'I WISH someone would come by and turn me on.' What if they don't show up? You've got to have a better plan for your life." — Jim Rohn

"WHEN PEOPLE ARE WORKING FOR THE MOTIVES OF SOMEONE ELSE, they profess not to understand or accept why things are done in the way they are. For anyone to feel responsible for their actions, they must sense the behavior has flowed from themselves." — Stanley Milgram

22. STRENGTHS VS WEAKNESSES INTERVIEW QUESTIONS

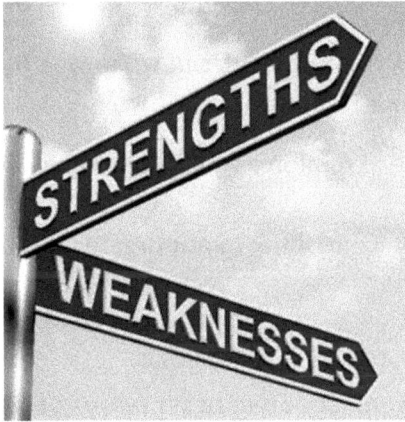

There are *many* questions an Interviewer can ask you about your strengths.

I've commented on a few of them, but the *main* concept is you share your responses in a *thoughtful* manner that highlights you well, but not at the expense of someone else.

- **Why should we hire you?**

BE CAREFUL WITH YOUR ANSWER HERE.

It isn't a time to be flippant. Saying "That you'd be stupid not to" won't help you.

However, this is a good time to remind the interviewer what you do have to offer.

- **What are your three greatest strengths?**

YOUR RESPONSE TO THIS SHOULD TIE IN WITH YOUR SUMMARY Statement from your resume.

It's another chance to reinforce what you have to offer.

- **What can you contribute to our organization?**

THIS IS WHERE HAVING A GOOD UNDERSTANDING OF THE organization's history and culture would come in.

You could align yourself with a cause they believe in.

- **Assume that you are a candidate in the coming general election. Tell me why you are the best candidate in the field.**

LET'S HOPE YOU DON'T GET ASKED THIS ONE, UNLESS YOU ACTUALLY ARE applying for a position within a political party.

This question is likely asking several things beneath the surface. How confident are you? Can you be self-promoting yet humble at the same time?

It also addresses how you speak about the competition.

HERE ARE SOME MORE EXAMPLES OF STRENGTH TYPE QUESTIONS:

- What is your greatest strength?

- We've interviewed a number of highly qualified students for this position. What sets you apart from the others?

- What are your strengths?

- Select four to five strengths that are *job-related*, highlighting technical and leadership skills and work ethic.

- What part of your current job are you the most comfortable with?

PRESUMABLY, YOUR *STRENGTHS* ARE WHAT HELPS YOU BECOME comfortable with a specific aspect of your *current* job.

Think of some examples that highlight your strengths. Perhaps you are good at customer service and working with people. Not everybody is.

Some people are more comfortable working with numbers. If that is your case, find a way to highlight the fact.

- **What are your strong points and how have they helped you to succeed?**

IN THIS NEXT SEGMENT, WE LOOK AT QUESTIONS THAT ADDRESS YOUR *weaknesses*.

You shouldn't feel intimidated about these questions.

We all have weaknesses.

Fortunately, we all have different weaknesses.

What really matters is you have *acknowledged* you aren't as strong in an area as you could be and that you are working on *improving* your skills and confidence in the area.

Whatever you come up with for an answer, you should probably find a way to tie it into the job position you are applying for.

Not the fact you are weak in the area but perhaps your willingness to *strengthen* your level of competency for the benefit of yourself and your new employer.

Here are a few personal weakness type questions.

They are all really variations on the same question.

- **What is your greatest weakness?**

MENTION ONE WORK-RELATED CHALLENGE THAT YOU ARE PREPARED TO overcome. For example: "I know there will be a learning curve before I am as productive as you would like a top performing (name of job you are applying for) to be. I have always been able to master the skills necessary to be successful, and I am confident I can do that working for (name of company)."

- **Name your three greatest weaknesses.**

- **Which is the worst of your three greatest weaknesses and why?**

- **What are your weaknesses?**

AND HERE'S SOME MORE...

- **What part of your current job are you the least comfortable with?**

- **What are your weak points and how have you overcome them?**

- **What about yourself would you want to improve?**

- **In which area do you need to make the improvement in?**

~

IN THE NEXT CHAPTER, WE LOOK AT QUESTIONS THAT ARE SPECIFIC TO interviewing for supervisory positions.

If you aren't applying for a supervisor's position, skip forward to the next chapter in this section.

"ATTITUDE PRECEDES SERVICE. YOUR POSITIVE MENTAL ATTITUDE IS THE basis for the way you act and react to people. 'You become what you think about' is the foundation of your actions and reactions. What are your thoughts? Positive all the time? How are you guiding them?" — Jeffrey Gitomer

23. SUPERVISOR ROLE SPECIFIC QUESTIONS

T he questions in this chapter, apply to job searchers who are applying for a supervisory position.

I'm not going to go into detail with these questions as they *likely* apply to a smaller group of job searchers than the general ones.

The questions are fairly specific, so you may want to spend some time on your own researching and developing some appropriate responses.

If you aren't applying for a supervisory position, please move on to the next chapter.

- **What is the purpose of a performance appraisal?**

- What is the most important quality a supervisor should have?
- An employee approaches you with a sexual harassment-related problem. In your discussion with the employee, what items of information will be of the most importance?
- What are the characteristics of an effective supervisor?
- What qualities make for a good boss?
- What steps can a supervisor take to improve the capabilities of staff?
- How should an assignment be made to an employee?
- How would a supervisor evaluate an administrative employee's performance?
- What are the three most common weaknesses of managers and supervisors?
- Why is feedback important?
- What are some of the ways in which an employee starts to behave that usually indicate a potential problem?
- What guidelines should be followed in counselling an employee?
- Name the major sources of conflict in organizations.
- Describe the process by which conflict in an organization should be addressed.
- What are the five functions of a supervisor?
- What considerations should be made in establishing organizational goals for your unit?
- What actions can a supervisor take to insure that subordinates support the mission and goals of an organization?
- Vacations during the holidays are popular among employees. Describe the actions a supervisor can take to insure that service levels are unaffected during these times.
- What are guidelines to follow in constructively criticizing an employee?

- **What are some of the signs that your staff may be suffering from burnout?**

[Declining health, increasing sickness and tardiness, absentminded-ness, flaring tempers and procrastination.]

∾

IN THE NEXT CHAPTER, WE LOOK AT **GET TO KNOW YOU** TYPE questions.

24. PERSONAL 'GET TO KNOW YOU' TYPE INTERVIEW QUESTIONS

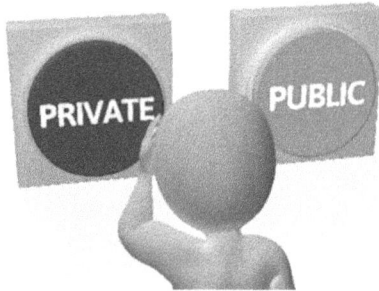

This chapter deals with Personal 'Get to Know You' Type Interview Questions.

As you would suspect, there are no right or wrong answers to these.

The purpose would seem to be for the Interviewer to take a *reading* on you as a person, separate from your work life. This would be *subjective* on their part of course.

For responding to these questions, you will want to be *upbeat*, *positive-thinking* and as always... show yourself in a good light.

Be careful of what some of us call *TMI* ... too much information. You don't want to provide so much information the Interviewer will start thinking about follow-up questions to what you have provided.

"Why in the world did you ever do that?" comes to mind.

I'm just going to list them and you can develop your own answers.

- **Tell us about the passion in your life as it relates to your work.**
- **What aspects of your work do you get the most excited about?**
- **What are your most outstanding qualities?**
- **If you were to start your own company, what would that company do?**
- **Tell me about the last book that you read.**
- **If you were a cucumber in a salad and somebody was about to eat you, what would you do?**

THIS LAST ONE HAS TO BE ONE OF THE STUPIDEST INTERVIEW QUESTIONS I've heard.

But you need to be prepared for questions that seem to come from outer space.

- **What are your worst qualities?**

IT MIGHT BE A GOOD OPPORTUNITY TO SAY YOU DON'T TASTE VERY GOOD in a salad with regards to the previous question, but you may want avoid it.

- **What is your favourite colour and what does it reflect in your personality?**

- Rate yourself from one to ten on your work ethic with ten being the best. Describe yourself.
- How would your friends describe you?
- Do you like to socialize outside of work?
- What are your hobbies?

IN THE NEXT CHAPTER, WE LOOK AT ILLEGAL INTERVIEW QUESTIONS AND how to answer them, or not!

"ACHIEVEMENT REQUIRES MORE THAN A VISION - IT TAKES COURAGE, resolve and tenacity." — Neil Eskelin

"SPECTACULAR ACHIEVEMENT IS ALWAYS PRECEDED BY SPECTACULAR preparation." -- Robert H. Schuller

25. ILLEGAL INTERVIEW QUESTIONS

I nterviewing job applicants has likely been with us *forever*.

OVER THE PAST 40 YEARS OR SO WITH THE DEVELOPMENT OF HUMAN rights, there has been a development in the area of what *kinds* of questions and *specific* questions Interviewers are able to ask you.

It can vary from country to country, so you would be *well advised* to do your own research to find out how things stand in your country.

These samples are provided for illustrative purpose only... drawn from Canadian and American resources and should not be considered as facts in law.

If you are interested in furthering your knowledge of questions that are appropriate vs illegal I would suggest you research the Human Rights Commission in the province or state that you live in.

What can you do if you are asked an illegal question?

If you're asked an illegal question, you have several options available to you.

You can choose to answer the question and that is well within your rights, but you can also refuse to answer as well.

Of course, taking this option may create a rift between you and the Interviewer.

However, if you choose to answer an illegal question, remember you are giving information that isn't related to the job; in fact, you might be giving the "wrong" answer, which could harm your chances of getting the job.

You can *refuse* to answer the question, which is well within your rights.

Unfortunately, depending on how you phrase your refusal, you run the *risk* of coming off as *uncooperative* or *confrontational* - hardly words an employer would use to describe the *"ideal"* candidate.

You can examine the question for its *intent* and *respond* with an answer as it might apply to the job.

For example, the Interviewer asks, "Are you a Canadian/US citizen?" or "What country are you from?"

You've been asked an illegal question.

You could respond, however, with "I am *authorized* to work in the USA." [or whatever country you live in]

Similarly, let's say the Interviewer asks, "Who is going to take care of your children when you have to travel for the job?"

You might answer, "I can *meet* the *travel* and *work* schedule this job requires."

If you can't see the *intent* behind the question, then ask "Can you tell me how this relates to my ability to fill the position?"

Most (if not all) interviewers will reword the question as it *relates* to the position.

You can also *choose to inform* the Interviewer the question they asked is illegal.

It's entirely possible the Interviewer was not aware of this fact or they may have just awkwardly phrased a *perfectly* legal question.

There is also the chance calling out a potential employer might make the interview process go worse, but you may not want to work for an organization that bases employment on inappropriate questions.

Please locate the Handout entitled *Interview Questions–Legal vs Illegal* located in the Additional Resources section at the end of the book for more detail.

It addresses specific areas of questioning that are illegal to ask and how it could or should be asked.

We won't be discussing it here.

"WHEN EVERYTHING SEEMS TO BE GOING AGAINST YOU, REMEMBER THE **airplane takes off against the wind, not with it.**" -- Henry Ford

26. BE A STAR!

J ob interviewing techniques have continued to evolve over the years.

In earlier chapters, we have looked at different ways to answer interview questions and looked at some *specific* questions you might be asked.

We are now going to build upon those techniques with yet another one. That is, being prepared to be a *STAR*.

STAR is an interview response technique that can be used by job seekers.

The STAR interview response technique is a method for answering behavioural interview questions. Behavioural interview questions are questions about how you have behaved in the past.

Specifically, they are about how you have handled certain work situations.

Interviewers ask these questions to see if candidates have the skills and experiences required for the job. One good way for them to see if candidates have what it takes is to look at past examples of performance.

Competency questions make up a large part of most job interviews and from a company's point of view they allow an objective assessment of a candidate's experience and the qualities that make them suitable for the job.

The STAR technique of interviewing makes it easier for the employer to compare all the people who are applying for the job in a methodical and structured way.

Here are some examples of behavioral interview questions. We will look at more examples later on:

• Tell me about a time you had to complete a task under a tight deadline.

• Have you ever gone above and beyond the call of duty?

• What do you do when a team member refuses to complete his or her portion of the work?

By now you are probably wondering what STAR stands for?

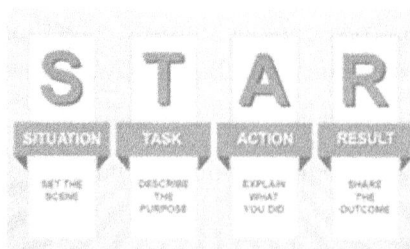

STAR is an acronym for four key concepts.

Each concept is a step the job candidate can take to answer a behavioural interview question.

By completing all four steps, the job candidate provides a thorough answer.

The concepts in the acronym include:

Situation: Describe a situation or problem you have encountered.

Task: Describe the task the situation required or your ideas for resolving the problem.

Action: Describe the action you took, obstacles that you had to overcome.

Results: Highlight outcomes achieved.

We'll expand upon each of these steps in a moment.

Which questions need a STAR response?

The questions will usually start along the lines of "tell me about a time when you..."

This will be followed by those competencies that have been listed on the job specification, so it is important to be familiar with them, so you can prepare.

For example, a marketing executive may require problem-solving skills, or a job in customer services may require conflict management skills. That would mean if you were applying for those jobs you would be well-advised to prepare answers to questions designed to determine whether you have the competency or not.

Hopefully, you do!

SOME INTERVIEWERS STRUCTURE THEIR QUESTIONS USING THE STAR technique. You may encounter a series of questions based around assessing one competency.

Here's a quick example: "Tell me about a time you had to complete a task under a tight deadline. Describe the situation and explain how you handled it."

Since you won't know in advance what interviewing techniques, your Interviewer will use, you'll benefit from preparing several scenarios from the jobs you've held.

First, make a list of the skills and/or experiences required for the job. You might look at the job listing for suggestions. Then, consider specific examples of times you displayed those skills.

For each example, name the *situation, task, action, and result.*

You can also look at common behavioral interview questions and try answering each of them using the *STAR* technique.

We'll provide a list of behavioral interview questions for you to practice on a little later.

Whatever examples you select, make sure they are as closely related to the job you're interviewing for as possible. Now, let's break the steps down into greater detail.

Situation:

This is about setting the scene, giving a context and background to the situation. This situation can be from a work experience, a volunteer position, or any other relevant event.

Be as specific as possible.

You must describe a specific event or situation, not a generalized description of what you have done in the past. Be sure to give enough detail for the interviewer to understand.

Describe the context within which you performed a job or faced a challenge at work. Make it *concise and informative*, concentrating solely on what is useful to the story.

For example, perhaps you were working on a group project, or you had a conflict with a co-worker.

So, if you're asked a question about time management, your reply would need to include the details of the project you were working on, who you were working with, when it happened and where you were.

As another example, if the question is asking you to describe a situation where you had to deal with a difficult person, explain how you came to meet that person and why they were being difficult.

If the question is asking for an example of teamwork, explain the task you had to undertake as a team.

Task

This is more *specific* to your exact role in the situation you are providing, so describe your responsibility in the situation.

You need to make sure the interviewer knows what you were tasked with rather than the rest of the team.

Examples: Perhaps you had to help your group complete a project under a tight deadline, or resolve a conflict with a co-worker.

Another... "It was my responsibility to find an alternative, so it didn't reflect badly on the company and we didn't waste the opportunity."

Action: This is the most important section of the STAR approach as it is where you will need to demonstrate and highlight the skills and personal attributes the question is testing i.e. what your response to the situation was.

Remember, you need to talk about what you specifically did, so using 'I' rather than team actions–otherwise you won't be showing off the necessary skills the employer is looking for.

Be sure to share a lot of detail, the interviewer will not be familiar with your history, although remember to avoid any acronyms and institutional language.

Now you have set the situation of your story, you need to explain what you did.

In doing so, you will need to remember the following:

• Be personal i.e. talk about you, not the rest of the team.

• Go into some detail.

• Do not assume they will guess what you mean.

• Avoid technical information, unless it is crucial to your story.

• Don't tell what you might do, explain what you did, how you did it, and why you did it.

What you're trying to get across here is how you assessed and decided what was the appropriate response to the situation and how you got the other team members involved–which in turn is a great way to demonstrate your communication skills.

What you did and how you did it.

The interviewers will want to know how you reacted to the situation.

This is where you can start selling some important skills you have.

For example, you may want to describe how you used the team to achieve a particular objective and how you used your communication skills to keep everyone updated on progress, etc.

Here's another example, if you are asked about dealing with a difficult personality on your team you would talk about how you decided to take a certain course of action to avoid making the situation worse or upsetting the individual.

Why you did it.

By highlighting the reasons behind your action, you would make a greater impact.

For example; when discussing a situation where you had to deal with conflict, many candidates would simply say: "I told my colleague to calm down and explained to him what the problem was.".

However, it would not provide a good idea of what drove you to act in this manner.

How did you ask him to calm down?

How did you explain the nature of the problem?

Here's an example of what you could say:

"I could sense my colleague was irritated, and I asked him gently to tell me what he felt the problem was.

By allowing him to express his feelings and his anger, I gave him the opportunity to calm down. I then explained to him my own point of view on the matter, emphasizing how important it was we found a solution that suited us both."

This revised answer helps the interviewers understand what drove your actions and reinforces the feeling you are calculating the consequences of your actions, thus retaining full control of the situation.

It provides much more information about you as an individual and is another reason why the STAR approach is so useful.

Result: Finally, explain the outcomes or results generated by the action taken. You might emphasize what you accomplished, or what you learned.

The result should be a positive one, and ideally one that can be quantified. Numbers always impress employers.

Examples of quantification, include repeat business, an increase in sales by 15% or saving the team 5 hours a week.

The Interviewer will also want to know what you learnt from that situation and if there was anything you'd do differently, the next time you were faced with the situation.

Here's an example, "Joseph didn't make the meeting on time, but we explained the problem to the 30 delegates and Frederick's presentation went well – a bit rough around the edges but it was warmly received.

Joseph managed to get there for the last 20 minutes to answer questions.

As a result, we gained some good contacts, at least two of which we converted into paying clients."

There are a few things to note with this response: it's important to speak in *specific* rather than *general* terms and *quantify* your success.

In this example, we mentioned 30 delegates, the names of the people involved and quantified two contacts converted to clients.

From a *listener*'s perspective, this makes the story more interesting and they are more able to gauge your success.

Nameless figures and *undefined* successes can make the answer less feel less convincing.

Secondly, as there are likely to be many questions and interviewers have short attention spans, it's important to keep your answers concise: convey the maximum achievement in the minimum time.

Finally, it's important to finish on a positive note so the overall impression is strong.

For a longer list of these types of questions, view the Behavioural-

Competency Based Interview Questions Handout, in the Additional Resources section.

∾

IN THE NEXT CHAPTER, WE DISCUSS QUESTIONS YOU CAN, SHOULD AND probably shouldn't ask your interviewer.

"THE ONLY REAL LIMITATION ON YOUR ABILITIES IS THE LEVEL OF YOUR desires. If you want it badly enough, there are no limits on what you can achieve." -- Brian Tracy

27. QUESTIONS TO ASK AN INTERVIEWER

In this chapter, we'll look at questions you can, should and probably shouldn't ask your interviewer.

Let's get started.

It's worth repeating... **Will Rogers** said, "I never met a man I didn't like."

AN EMPLOYMENT INTERVIEW IS A PLACE TO BE *LIKED*. UNLESS YOU'RE *likeable*, you won't be *hireable*.

LISTENING AND QUESTIONING PROPERLY IS THE WAY TO WIN THE interview. For the first few minutes of the interview, you're *observing* and *determining* how to proceed. You've been given *impossible* questions and have delivered *inspirational* answers.

NOW YOU MUST ASK QUESTIONS... *CAREFULLY*.

• • •

In the recruiter's rule book CLOSING ON OBJECTIONS, PAUL Hawkinson (1984) wrote:

Constant questioning can be grating, and if overused, can work against you.

No one wants to feel they are on the receiving end of the prosecutor's interrogation and questions must be used sparingly to be really effective.

But they are necessary because selling is the art of asking the right questions to get to the minor yes's that allow you lead... to the major decision and major yes.

The final placement is nothing more than the sum total of all your *yes's* throughout the process.

Your job then, is to nurse the process along.

That advice is written for Recruiters in their task of interviewing job applicants.

WHEN YOU ASK QUESTIONS OF THE INTERVIEWER, FOR THOSE BRIEF moments, you are the Interviewer and you don't want to put them on the defense.

But before we get into some techniques for making the sale i.e. landing the job, let's take a look at some questions you might ask your Interviewer.

They are meant to help you prepare for the interview.

Some questions *may or may not* be appropriate for your interviewing situation. While asking questions of your interviewer may help you look eager and enthusiastic, it may be a tactic to use with caution.

Your Interviewer has come prepared to ask *you* questions. They may not be prepared to respond to *your* questions. The last thing you want to do is to *intimidate* your Interviewer.

If you do ask your Interviewer questions, this is where your notebook might come in handy in recording your Interviewer's response.

LET'S LOOK AT SOME QUESTIONS:

Note: Indicates some background information or industry advice has been provided for you to consider.

- **Why is this position open?**
- **How often has it been filled in the past five years? What were the main reasons?**
- **What would you like done differently by the next person who fills this position?**
- **What are some objectives you would like to see accomplished in this job?**
- **What is most pressing? What would you like to have done in the next 3 months?**
- **What would you want the person in this position to accomplish the first 30 days on the job?** [Respond with excitement about working on the type of projects/assignments mentioned.]
- **What qualities are you seeking in top candidates for this position?**

[If the Interviewer lists a quality/strength you have, but have not covered during your interview, respond by letting the employer know you have that skill.]

[If the Interviewer mentions something that matched your discussion, you can respond you are pleased to hear they are seeking someone with your skills and abilities.]

- **What are some of the long-term objectives you would like to see completed?**

- What are some of the more difficult problems one would have to face in this position?
- What type of support does this position receive in terms of people, finances, etc.?
- What freedom would I have in determining my own work objectives, deadlines, and methods of measurement?
- What advancement opportunities are available for the person who is successful in this position, and within what time frame?
- In what ways has this organization been most successful in terms of products and services over the years?
- What significant changes do you foresee in the near future?
- How is one evaluated in this position?
- What accounts for success within the company?
- Are you *ready* and *able* to hire now?
- How long will it take to make a hiring decision?
- What is the next step in the hiring process?

[If the Interviewer's answer is vague, ask if you can follow up in a week. This question and response reinforces the fact you are very interested in the job.]

~

IN THE NEXT CHAPTER, WE LOOK AT USING A TECHNIQUE FROM THE SALES field to move your interview along. Hopefully, to the point you get offered the job.

28. USING "TIE DOWN" TECHNIQUES TO MOVE THE INTERVIEW ALONG

I n this chapter, we look at using "Tie Down" Techniques to Move the Interview Along, in your favour.

Moving the process along is done through the use of '**tie down**' phrases in questions designed to elicit an *affirmative* response.

The method comes from the sales field. You have likely had it used on *you* many times and haven't been aware of it. The idea is the sales person, in this case it's *you* trying to sell *yourself* as the best candidate for the job, tries to get the other person to answer '*yes*' to a series of small questions.

Once the person has answered 'yes' to the questions, it becomes very difficult for them to say 'no' to the big question.

Two challenges arise when using this technique.

Firstly, you need to get used to using it. I would suggest doing some role playing with a partner and try to sell them something. Doesn't matter what it is, it could be a pretend product, something you have made up.

The idea is to try to take the other person on a journey to the point where they have no choice but to buy your product or service.

The *second* challenge is you need to use this technique in a way the person isn't aware a technique is being used on them.

Most of us don't like to be sold to. We like to be helped to make a purchasing decision though.

We can use the same sales technique in moving our job interview along to the point where we will be offered the job.

Here are the most common techniques. I'm just going to comment on the ones that are likely usable in your job interview.

Aren't I/you/we/they?

Can't I/he/she/you/we/they/it?

Doesn't he/she/it?

Don't I/you/we/they?

Don't you agree?

Hasn't she/he/ it?

Haven't I/you/we/they?

Isn't he/she/it?

Isn't that right?

Shouldn't I/he/she/you/we/they/it?

Wasn't I /he/she/it?

Weren't you/we/they?

Won't I/he/she/you/we/they/ it?

Wouldn't I,/he/she/you/we/they/it?

There are many kinds of tie downs.

Now we are going to look at *four* of them that have value in moving *forward* in a job interview.

You should vary your dialogue when using them so you don't appear obvious or overbearing.

With each agreement, you obtain from the Interviewer, you have scored one more "minor yes" leading up to a "major yes" offer.

The Standard Tie Down: These are used at the *end* of a question:

"My qualifications appear to fit the position you have open, *don't they*?"

"Diversified Enterprises really has a lot to offer someone with my experience, *doesn't it?*"

"It looks like we'll be able to eliminate the problem, *don't you agree?*"

THE INVERTED TIE DOWN: THESE ARE USED AT THE *BEGINNING* OF A question:

"Isn't it an excellent position for someone with my background?"

"Don't you think we'll be working together well?"

THE INTERNAL TIE DOWN: THESE ARE USED IN THE *MIDDLE* OF A compound sentence:

"Now we have had the opportunity to meet, *wouldn't it* be great to work together?"

THE TAG-ON TIE DOWN: THE FINAL KIND OF TIE DOWN IS USED *AFTER* A statement of fact. A slight pause, then an emphasis on the tie down, improves it effect:

"My experience will benefit Diversified Enterprises, *won't it?"*

"You've really spent a lot of time and money to get the right person, *haven't you?"*

"This problem can be corrected easily, *can't it?"*

THE BEST WAY TO LEARN TIE DOWN QUESTIONING TECHNIQUES IS THE same way you rehearse your script for the interview.

You write down all the tie down lines you can use during the interview, then read them into a voice recorder and play them back once or twice a day, every day, to implant them into your subconscious.

They'll pop out automatically when you need them.

~

IN THE NEXT CHAPTER WE DISCUSS COMMON JOB INTERVIEW MISTAKES and how to prevent them from happening in the first place.

29. JOB SEARCH/INTERVIEW MISTAKES & HOW TO CORRECT THEM

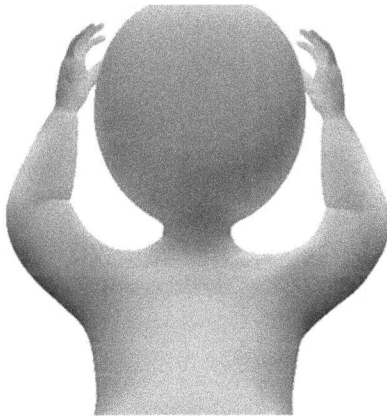

I n this chapter, we provide examples of common job interview mistakes and how to *prevent* them from *happening* in the first place.

At any given time, there are *countless* people who are looking for employment.

As we have advocated throughout this program, there are *right ways and wrong ways* to go about your job search. Yet so many people are still doing things that *hurt* their chances of finding employment.

You don't want to rub prospective employers the *wrong* way. After all, competition for jobs can be extremely *competitive*. Why reduce your chances of being selected as a successful candidate?

To help you put forth your best impression possible, here are some examples of job interview mistakes others have made. If *you* don't make them in the *first* place, you won't have to worry about how to correct them.

Common Job Interview Mistakes

- **When contacted for an interview, the applicant says they have no idea who the person calling is and asks what job this is.**

Ok, maybe in some extreme cases the applicant may have *forgotten* applying for the position. However, you should always pay attention to the job postings you apply for.

Make sure you keep a file of all the job advertisements you apply for as well as the cover letter you write for it (remember each job should get its own cover letter written specifically to the job requirements of the position and how you meet those requirements.)

Do some research on the company you are applying to and research what the position is so you are well-aware of the company or the position when you get a call for an interview.

- **The candidate shows up late for the interview.**

Being late for an interview? Really?

Things do happen but by all means give yourself enough time to arrive a little early for your interview.

First impressions are huge.

If you can't show up on time for the interview, how can the employer count on you, day to day in the job? No excuse (traffic back up, road construction, got lost, etc.) is going to change the poor first impression you've made.

Leave extra early to allow for any delays be ready to interview when you walk in the door. Map out your route on your phone so you know exactly where to go, what floor to go to and which person to ask for.

- **The candidate shows up too early.**

On the flip side, avoid showing up for the interview too early.

Why is this a problem?

Quite often interviews are scheduled back to back, and it is awkward for the Receptionist to have 2 or 3 people waiting for interviews. As well if you are the first interview of the day, the office may not be ready for you yet.

It is best you do arrive to the area early but only come into the building 5-10 minutes early prior to your interview.

- **The applicant brings too many items with them to the interview.**

Nothing is more distracting, unprofessional and disorganized than when you arrive juggling your cell phone, a Starbucks or Tim Hortons coffee cup, a huge purse/backpack/briefcase, an umbrella and a coat!

Be prepared and arrive with only the essentials you need to participate in the interview.

Ideally, you will want to arrive with only your car keys, your phone (more on that in a second) and a small folder or briefcase (that contains your resume, references, cover letter, the job advertisement, company information and some questions you may have about the company or position).

Leave all unnecessary baggage hidden in your vehicle and arrive composed and ready to participate in your interview.

- **The applicant is texting or on the phone.**

We get it; we are a plugged-in world, but by all means, ignore your phone for 30-60 minutes when you are in your interview.

Turn it off, ensure your ringer is off and maybe better yet leave your phone in your purse, backpack or briefcase. There is nothing more annoying than your phone ringing or buzzing during a meeting... interviews are no exception.

Shut off your cell phone before you get to the interview.

- **The candidate is chewing gum, candy or carrying a coffee.**

This is very unprofessional and far too casual behavior. Spit out your gum into a garbage can before you get to the building and get a coffee after the interview.

If you are offered a beverage during the interview, by all means accept it, but don't bring your own.

- **Candidate wears strong perfume/cologne/scents or smokes right before the interview.**

You want to be conscious of how many people have allergies to scents or asthma sensitivities.

You also want to make a great first impression and sending the receptionist or Interviewer into an allergic reaction is not going to help.

For you smokers out there, while you may not be able to smell the smoke and nicotine emanating from your person, others can. Try to avoid lighting up before an interview.

- **Research the parking situation.**

Prior to arriving be sure to know where you can park and if you need to pay for parking. Make sure you plug the parking meter sufficiently. Have an idea of how long your interview is expected to take and put more money in the meter than you need.

You don't want to have to interrupt the interview to go plug the parking meter, so be prepared ahead of time.

- **Applicant dresses inappropriately.**

Depending on the type of job being applied for, your attire may vary. Regardless, you should dress professionally without overdressing for your interview.

Mini-skirts, impractical high heels, or casual, immodest or flashy clothing will set the wrong impression. For any professional position, erring on the side of modesty will always help make the right impression.

If you are serious about finding a good job for yourself, you will take each chance you need to make an excellent impression. Applicants lose the interest of employers if they are unprofessional or casual.

- **Candidate talks too much.**

Interviews should involve two-way dialogue.

While the *employer* is looking to learn more about you, avoid *dominating* the conversation and not letting the Interviewer get a word in. Listen *carefully* and provide a *clear concise* response to questions.

Use your judgement as to when you need to communicate additional details.

Being confident is one thing but being a chatty pants can be annoying and may impact the first impression you are presenting.

- **Fuzzy Resume Facts**

Even if you have submitted a resume when you applied for the job, you may also be asked to fill out a job application during your interview.

Make sure you know the information you will need to complete an application including dates of prior employment, graduation dates and employer contact information. It's understandable that some of your older experiences may be hard to recall.

Review the facts before your interview. It can be helpful to keep a copy of your resume for yourself to refer to during your interview although certainly don't use it as a crutch.

- **Not Paying Attention**

Don't let yourself zone out during an interview. Make sure you are well-rested, alert and prepared for your interview.

Getting distracted and missing a question looks bad on your part. If you zone out, your potential employer will wonder how you will be able to stay focused during a day on the job, if you can't even focus during one interview.

If you feel your attention slipping away, make the effort to stay engaged. Maintain eye contact, lean forward slightly when talking to your Interviewer and make an active effort to listen effectively.

While you may have no problem paying attention in a one-on-one interview in a private office, it's harder to stay in tune with the interviewer when you're meeting in a public place.

- **Not Being Prepared to Answer Questions**

Your Interviewer is probably going to ask you more than just the basics about where you worked, and when.

To get a feel of your aptitude for a job, your Interviewer is going to take advantage of the allotted time and flesh out everything he or she needs to know about you as an employee.

Don't let yourself be caught off guard. Prepare for your interview by reviewing what questions to expect, and how to answer them.

Be prepared with a list of questions to ask the employer so you're ready when you asked if you have questions for the Interviewer.

- **Not having any questions**

Most Interviewers leave time at the end to answer questions. Usually, they know you're vetting them, too, and want to make sure it's a two-sided conversation.

It's also a bit of a test.

The questions you ask often reveal the way you think and what's important to you. It also shows you care enough about the job that you want to know more.

Not having any questions prepared, signals you don't care, aren't curious, or haven't done your homework.

If you freeze up, throw out an old standby question like, "What does success look like in this role?" or "What's the culture like here?"

- **Asking weirdly personal questions**

Conversely, some candidates get a little too personal with their questions.

Your questions should be related to the job in discussion, not related to the interviewer.

- **Badmouthing Past Employers**

Don't make the mistake of badmouthing your boss or coworkers.

It's sometimes a smaller world than you think and you don't know who your Interviewer might know, including your former boss who is an idiot...

You also don't want the Interviewer to think you might speak that way about his or her company if you leave on terms that aren't the best.

When interviewing for a job, you want your employer to know you can work well with other people and handle conflicts in a mature and effective way, rather than badmouthing your coworkers or talking about other's incompetence.

When you're asked hard questions, like "Tell me about a time you didn't work well with a supervisor. What was the outcome and how would you have changed the outcome?"

or "Have you worked with someone you didn't like? If so, how did you handle it?," don't fall back on badmouthing other people. Instead, review how to answer difficult questions.

- **Displaying low energy**

This one is hard to define but an interview killer.

Here's what it looks like: Slumped shoulders, lack of eye contact, slowness to respond to questions and a general lack of enthusiasm for the company or role.

If you don't clearly want the job, it's near impossible to persuade someone to give it to you.

- **Focusing too much on themselves**

Talking endlessly about what you want, how this job is the direction you want to go in your career and how the experience would be great for you is meaningless drivel to an Interviewer.

Companies don't pay you to help you out!

They hire you because you have traits and skills that will help them achieve their goals. Use your responses to illustrate how you can be of service to the hiring manager.

- **Forgetting to follow up**

So many people forget this basic rule of interviewing: Follow up within 24 hours by email to thank the Interviewer for their time and underscore your interest in the position.

If you don't do it, hiring managers may think you're not interested or organized, or they may simply forget about you.

- **Following up too aggressively**

While it's important to follow up, you should not send multiple emails or call an Interviewer.

It is extremely awkward for Employers to receive a call out of the blue from someone demanding to know why they haven't heard from them.

Send your follow-up email and then move on with your life. Anything more is probably too much.

- **Being angry**

Angry people are NOT people employers want to hire.

Angry people are not fun to work with. They may frighten co-workers and/or customers or clients. They may also abuse both people and equipment (computers, cars, etc.).

Instead: If you are angry over a job loss, horrible commute to the interview, earlier fight with your kids or spouse, or anything else, dump the anger before the interview, at least temporarily.

Stop, before you enter the employer's premises, take a few deep breaths, put a smile on your face and do your best to switch gears mentally so you are not "in a bad place" in your mind.

- **Sharing TMI (too much information)**

Sometimes, people have a whole-truth-and-nothing-but-the-truth mindset in a job interview, so they "spill their guts" in answer to every question. Not smart or useful!

We're not recommending telling any lies, but we are recommending you avoid boring the interviewer and blowing an opportunity by sharing too much information.

If they want more details, they'll ask.

Instead: Answer their question and then stop talking. Or, ask a question of your own.

- **Negative body language**

If you never smile, have a limp handshake, and don't make eye contact with the people you meet at the employer's location and especially with the Interviewer, you'll come across as too shy or too strange or simply not interested.

Instead: Show your interest and enthusiasm.

- **Flirting or other inappropriate behavior**

Unless you are interviewing for a job as a comedian or host/hostess in a social club, don't try to be entertaining or amusing.

And, don't flirt with anyone, including the receptionist and the security guard.

Instead: If making them laugh isn't a requirement of the job, take the interview seriously.

Save flirting for your second day of work.

- **Not having an elevator pitch.**

Likely, in every interview, you'll encounter some variation of the "tell me about yourself" prompt.

This is a direct invitation to outshine your resume, tell the employer what value you're bringing to the table, and address any weaknesses or anomalies in your employment or educational record.

Too many people think they'll be able to "wing" this part of the interview, but scientifically, it's just not possible:

The average human attention span is five seconds, so if you aren't ready to go when the moment comes, you'll lose the Interviewer's interest in the time it takes you to craft a response.

This completely defeats the purpose of the elevator pitch, which is to start - not conclude - the conversation.

- **Asking for feedback after being rejected.**

Requesting feedback or suggestions for improvement may demonstrate your humility and dedication to personal growth, but it puts the hiring manager in an awkward position.

Furthermore, it's unlikely you'll get a straightforward response, because most feedback can create a legal liability for the employer.

Additionally, and perhaps most importantly, responding to requests for feedback takes up time the employer doesn't have, which is often seen as intrusive and irritating.

So, please, reconsider asking for it.

Note: This is another one of those controversial suggestions. Other experts will tell you that you should follow-up with rejections.

You may learn some valuable information for your next interview.

- **Missing Opportunities to Prove Yourself.**

Interviewers will ask questions that give you the chance to demonstrate your qualifications and show you have what it takes to do the job.

"Failure to answer questions with ESR (Example, Specifics, Results) responses," is a failure to make the most of the interview.

Most questions offer you the opportunity in your answer to provide the Interviewer with specific, relevant examples of you accomplishing some type of measurable result that benefited the employer.

This requires you to have done your homework ahead of time and to accurately portray what happened, so when the employer verifies your story with prior employers, it matches what you said.

- **Begging for the job**

Even if you are desperate for work, begging won't help.

You will probably embarrass your Interviewer and will lower your chances of being considered for the job.

I personally have experienced this when I was hiring to fill a position.

- **Forgetting to notify your references you have just had an interview and the employer may be calling**

It can be a waste of an Interviewer's time and effort to contact one of your references only to find out they didn't know that they were a reference or they didn't know much about you.

Securing a job interview should be considered as a success, but it is often just the first step in the process.

In order to make a great impression you will want to avoid the job interview mistakes listed above. Be prepared, project confidence and be professional.

A mediocre interview can make or break your chances of a second interview or of receiving an offer.

∾

IN OUR NEXT CHAPTER WE TAKE A BRIEF LOOK AT MAKING A POST-interview phone call.

"NO ONE LIMITS YOUR GROWTH BUT YOU. IF YOU WANT TO EARN MORE, **learn more. That means you'll work harder for a while; that means you'll work longer for a while. But you'll be paid for your extra effort with enhanced earnings down the road." -- Tom Hopkins**

30. MAKING THE FOLLOW-UP
PHONE CALL

Assuming you have made it to the interview stage, here is a strategy to consider after your interview.

The follow-up telephone call is one of the most *important devices* in job searching and also one of the *most unused*.

Many job searchers *don't* feel confident enough about themselves to make this important phone call.

As with your initial follow-up response, the keys to success when you telephone your target are *timing* and *technique*. That means knowing:

- When to call
- Whom to call

- And What to say

YOUR ONGOING PURPOSE OF THIS *FOLLOW-UP* PHONE CALL IS TO maintain the prospect's impression of you as:

- Enthusiastic
- Confident
- Energetic
- Dependable
- Loyal
- Honest
- Proud of your work
- Concerned with service

THE FACT YOU'RE TAKING THE *TROUBLE* TO MAKE THIS FOLLOW-UP CALL, by itself, *demonstrates* these qualities.

Or at least it should!

Let's look at timing the Telephone Follow-up.

Don't Wait Too Long!

The best advice to heed is the "fiddle theory," introduced by Robert Singer in Winning Through Intimidation:

The longer a person *fiddles* around with something, the greater the odds that the result will be negative...

In the case of *Nero*, Rome burned; in the case of a *sale*, the longer it takes to get to a point of closing, the greater the odds it will *never* close.

As a *general* rule, you should always assume time is always against you when you try to make a deal --- *any* kind of deal.

There's an old saying about "striking while the iron's hot."

If you haven't received a response to your follow-up letter within a *week* after the interview, call, but ... Never on a Monday.

Mondays are full of staff meetings, unexpected crises, and weekend wounds. Don't call, write, or interview on a Monday if you can help it.

Statistically, the best time to call is Tuesday through Friday, from 9.00 am to 11.00 am.

TARGETING THE TELEPHONE FOLLOW-UP

You *already* know who should receive your call.

You spent a long time talking with him or her during the first interview.

Despite these interview tips, you may still feel in a one-down position with your Interviewer. Don't!

Initiating the call automatically gives you the upper hand.

You're *prepared* and can *guide* the conversation to the outcome you want.

SECTION FOUR: ADDITIONAL RESOURCES

Here is a collection of job interview preparation related questions asked on Quora.com and answered by me, Rae Stonehouse.

It's cumbersome to add hyperlinks in this printed version, so I haven't.

If you would like to read more answers to the questions, from people who may or may not agree with me... and some... who may be from outer space and worth a chuckle, just visit Quora and enter the title of the question into their search bar.

~

31. WHOLE LOTTA SHAKING GOING ON

I've titled this chapter **Whole Lotta Shaking Going On**, because when you are out there networking, meeting new people and greeting people you already know, there *really* is a lot of hand shaking going on.

A handshake is more than just a greeting. It is also a message about your personality and confidence level.

In business, a handshake is an important tool in making the right first impression. The same applies when you are job searching.

Your *business* is finding yourself a job.

Let's take a closer look at the simple act of shaking another's hand. Maybe, it's not so simple after all!

Before extending your hand, introduce yourself. Extending your hand should be part of an introduction, not a replacement for using your voice.

This isn't the cue to start reciting your elevator pitch though.

Extending your hand without saying anything may make you appear nervous or overly aggressive. On one hand (pun intended!) it would seem that shaking someone's hand should be an easy process. We have likely been doing it most of our adult life.

On the other hand, some people seem to have problems with it.

I believe that part of the problem that creates anxiety is that we over think things sometimes. We are anxious because we give more importance to the activity than it really deserves and it takes on a life of its own, creating anxiety.

A self-fulfilling prophesy if there ever was one.

Another part that likely creates anxiety is that we can only control our portion of the interaction. If our partner is an experienced hand-shaker, then all should go smoothly but many aren't.

THERE ARE A FEW *DIffERENT* HAND-SHAKING STYLES THAT COME UP IN the liter- ature and I am sure you have likely experienced them yourselves.

I personally don't like grasping someone's hand who has the so-called "**wet fish**" handshake. It can leave you with an obsessive urge to wipe your hand as soon as you can, but fight the urge.

Even worse, there are times that my hand is sweating and I don't want the label. I have developed the habit of giving my hand a quick, unobtrusive wipe on my pant leg before offering my hand.

THEN THERE IS "**BONE-CRUSHER BILL.**" THE OFFERED HAND OFTEN comes in as curve from the hip of Bill with the express purpose of crushing walnuts.

Or so it would seem.

Bill never seems to realize the pain that he causes in others or the fact that people start to avoid him. Word can get around!

· · ·

Another ineffective handshake I call the "Royal" handshake.

Someone only offers you the tips of their fingers and no matter how you try you can't seem to grasp more than a few fingers. You are left feeling that you were robbed.

The bottom line is that *you* should avoid being any of these profiles. If you need to practice at home before going to a networking session, do so.

It seems to be coming more common that friends are hugging when meeting in a social setting. There are many people that are what I call "huggy" people.

I would suggest waiting to see if you offered one rather than expecting one. It could make for an awkward situation if you were to offer a hug on a first contact and it wasn't welcomed.

∿

32. YOUR USP

Your **unique selling proposition** (a.k.a. **unique selling point**, universal selling point or **USP**) is a marketing concept used to differentiate yourself from your competitors or others in the market place.

Some good current examples of products with a clear USP are:

- Head & Shoulders: "You get rid of dandruff"

Some unique propositions that were pioneers when they were introduced:

- Domino's Pizza: "You get fresh, hot pizza delivered to your door in 30 minutes or less—or it's free."
- FedEx: "When your package absolutely, positively has to get there overnight"
- M&M's: "Melts in your mouth, not in your hand"
- Metropolitan Life: "Get Met, It Pays"

The term USP has been largely replaced by the concept of a *Posi-*

tioning Statement. Positioning is determining what place a brand (tangible good or service) should occupy in the consumer's mind in comparison to its competition. A position is often described as the meaningful difference between the brand and its competitors.
Source: Wikipedia

I recently was blindsided at a Chamber of Commerce function in my city when we were standing in circle participating in what they call a power networking session. We were asked what makes us or our business unique. I didn't recognize it as a USP question and provided an ineffective response. If I had recognized it for what it was i.e. a USP question I would have responded with "Mr. Emcee is a full-service event organizer. From start to finish ... we do it all!"

Your challenge is to develop a USP that on one hand is short and to the point, yet is clear enough that it captures the essence of your business and will stick in the mind of whoever you are sharing it with. Having it prepared in advance, believing in it and being able to recite it with a moment's notice will go a long way in reducing your anxiety and fear which are all part of shyness.

I would also suggest researching your competitors or others that are in a similar business that are not necessarily your competitors to see if they have chosen a similar USP as you have. I am aware of two business coaches that chose a USP that had only one word that was different. That one word totally changed the context of the USP but it really upset one of the coaches accusing the other of stealing her idea, even though they had been developed independent of each other.

Power Networking Logistics:

1. Research your competitors to learn what their USPs are.
2. Create a USP for your business.
3. Share it with colleagues and ask their opinion. Ask if it makes sense. Ask if it is easy to understand. Ask if it captures the essence of your business.

WHAT DO YOU STAND FOR?

_____

What is your USP?

_____

33. LEGAL VS ILLEGAL JOB INTERVIEW QUESTIONS HANDOUT

Note: this document is written from the perspective of an Employer

INQUIRY AREA

Illegal Questions

NATIONALITY ORIGIN/CITIZENSHIP

- Are you a Canadian/American citizen?
- Where were you/your parents born?
- What is your "native tongue"?
- Are you authorized to work in Canada?
- What language do you read/ speak/write fluently? (This question is okay only if this ability is relevant to the performance of the job.)

Age

- How old are you?
- When did you graduate?
- What's your birth date?
- Are you between the ages of 18 and 64?

Marital/Family Status

- What's your marital status?
- Whom do you live with?
- Do you plan to have a family? When?
- How many kids do you have?
- What are your child-care arrangements?
- Would you be willing to relocate if necessary?
- Would you be able and willing to travel as needed by the job? (This question is okay if it is asked of all applicants for the job.)
- Would you be able and willing to work overtime as necessary? (Again, this question is okay assuming it is asked of all applicants for the job.)

Affiliations

- What clubs or social organizations do you belong to?
- List any professional or trade groups or other organizations that you belong to that you consider relevant to your ability to perform this job.

Personal

- How tall are you? How much do you weigh? (Questions about height & weight are not acceptable unless minimum standards are essential to the safe performance of the job.)
- Are you able to lift a 30kg weight and carry it 100 metres/300 feet, as that is part of the job?

Disabilities

- Do you have any disabilities?
- Please complete the following medical history:
- Have you had any recent or past illnesses or operations? (If yes, list them and give dates when these occurred.)
- What was the date of your last physical exam?
- How's your family's health?
- When did you lose your eyesight? How?
- Do you need an accommodation to perform the job? (This question can only be asked after a job offer has been made.)
- Are you able to perform the essential functions of this job? (This question is okay if the interviewer has thoroughly described the job.)
- Can you demonstrate how you would perform the following job-related functions?
- As part of the hiring process, after a job offer has been made, you will be required to undergo a Medical exam. (Exam results must be kept strictly confidential, except medical/safety personnel may be informed if emergency medical treatment is required, and supervisors may be informed about necessary job accommodations, based on exam results.)

Arrest Record

- Have you ever been arrested?
- Have you ever been convicted of _____? (The crime named should be reasonably related to the performance of the job in question.)

Sex

- Are you male or female?

- What are the names & Relationships of persons living with you?
- You may be asked if you have ever worked under another name.

Race/Colour

- What is your race? What colour is your hair, eyes, or skin?
- No race-related questions are legal.

Religion

- What is your religious affiliation or denomination?
- What church do you belong to?
- What is the name of your pastor, minister, or rabbi?
- What religious holidays do you observe?
- None (If you wish to know if an applicant is available to work Saturday or Sunday shifts, ask: "Are you available to work on Saturdays and Sundays if needed?" Make sure you ask this question of all applicants.)

34. BEHAVIORAL/COMPETENCY BASED INTERVIEW QUESTIONS HANDOUT

Note: At the end of each example there is a notation of what competency the question is assessing.

1. Describe a situation in which you had to use reference materials to write a research paper. What was the topic? What journals did you read? (research/written communication)

2. Give me a specific example of a time when a co-worker or classmate criticized your work in front of others. How did you respond? How has that event shaped the way you communicate with others? (oral communication)

3. Give me a specific example of a time when you sold your supervisor or professor on an idea or concept. How did you proceed? What was the result? (assertiveness)

4. Describe the system you use for keeping track of multiple projects. How do you track your progress so that you can meet deadlines? How do you stay focused? (commitment to task)

5. Tell me about a time when you came up with an innovative solution to a challenge your company or class was facing.

What was the challenge? What role did others play? (creativity & imagination)

6. Describe a specific problem you solved for your employer or professor. How did you approach the problem? What role did others play? What was the outcome? (decision making)

7. Describe a time when you got co-workers or classmates who dislike each other to work together. How did you accomplish this? What was the outcome? (teamwork)

8. Tell me about a time when you failed to meet a deadline. What things did you fail to do? What were the repercussions? What did you learn? (time management)

9. Describe a time when you put your needs aside to help a co-worker or classmate understand a task. How did you assist them? What was the result? (flexibility)

10. Describe two specific goals you set for yourself and how successful you were in meeting them. What factors led to your success in meeting your goals?

11. Tell me about a time in which you had to use your written communication skills in order to get across an important point. (Decision Making)

12. Give me an example of a time you had to make a difficult decision. (Decision Making)

13. Describe a specific problem you solved for your employer. How did you approach the problem? What role did others play? What was the outcome?

14. Give me an example of when taking your time to make a decision paid off. (Initiative)

15. What did you do to prepare for this interview?

16. Give me an example of a situation that could not have happened successfully without you being there. (Planning & Organization)

17. Describe a situation when you had many projects due at the same time. What steps did you take to get them all done?

18. How do you determine priorities in scheduling your time? Give me an example. (Flexibility)

19. Describe a time where you were faced with problems or stresses that tested your coping skills.
20. Describe a time when you put your needs aside to help a co-worker understand a task. How did you assist them? What was the result? (Leadership)
21. Tell me about a time when you influenced the outcome of a project by taking a leadership role. (Leadership)
22. Give me an example of when you involved others in making a decision. (Time Management)
23. Tell me about a time when you failed to meet a deadline. What things did you fail to do? What were the repercussions? What did you learn?
24. Tell me about a time when you were particularly effective on prioritizing tasks and completing a project on schedule.

35. QUESTION: IS IT OKAY TO FAKE A RESPONSE ON AN INTERVIEW JUST TO GIVE A GOOD IMPRESSION?

A nswer Provided:

No, DEFINITELY NOT. YOU ARE ONLY FOOLING YOURSELF IF YOU THINK you are fooling your Interviewer.

Most interviewers, if they have experience, will know they are being fed a line. This only sets them up for thinking "I wonder what else you are lying about"?

I believe you are far better to admit you don't know anything about the question being asked. An alternative, if you don't know a lot about the question, is to respond with what you do know about it. That's not the same as faking it.

You will probably get a better impression by admitting you don't know something than faking it and proving you don't know something.

As originally answered on Quora.com.

~

36. QUESTION: IF A JOB APPLICANT MENTIONED USING INFORMAL MINDFULNESS MEDITATIONS (IN THE INTEREST SECTION) AS AN EFFECTIVE CONCENTRATION AID ON A CV, IS IT LIKELY A POTENTIAL EMPLOYER WOULD SEE THIS AS A VALUABLE THING?

A nswer Provided:

I had to reread the original question after reading some of the answers provided.

I thought the question was asking about 'mindfulness medications' which takes the question in a different direction. To that question I would have replied 'No, definitely not!'

In my humble opinion, I don't see the value in adding mention of using any sort of meditation on your CV. Nor do I see the value of adding an Interest section.

You would be better off expanding other sections of your CV/resume to show you are the best candidate for the job. And what you do include on your resume should directly relate to the requirements of the job and your ability to fulfill them.

I believe an Interest section is just fluff on a CV. Don't get me wrong, there is value in having a repertoire of interests to share and demonstrate your passion, but save it for your interview where you can wow the Interviewer with your passions in life help make you a good hire.

37. QUESTION: DOES IT MAKE YOU UNEASY TO INTERVIEW FOR AN EXPERIENCED, MID-LEVEL POSITION THAT HAS BEEN OPEN FOR 60 DAYS OR MORE?

Answer Provided:

I don't see myself applying for an experienced, mid-level position in the near future.

Having said that, I wouldn't see myself worrying the position has been open for 60 days or more.

It often takes a while for an employer to get things organized. There may not have been any qualified applicants. The fact that you are being interviewed at all is noteworthy in the sense that they are considering you as a potential hire.

There may even be other reasons such as nobody wants to apply for the job. There could be a myriad of problems with the job, including the direct supervisor, the employees, working conditions, etc.

It might be worth your while to do some sleuthing to find out if any of what I have suggested may be true. If they are, it may be a deal breaker for you wanting to work there. Or, it may give you some insight on how to answer questions from the interviewer that may be covertly addressing a problematic work environment.

As originally answered on Quora.com.

38. QUESTION: IS IT A BAD IDEA TO POSTPONE A JOB INTERVIEW (RIGHT AWAY) BECAUSE OF YOUR CURRENT JOB?

Answer Provided:

While it has been proposed that you should never turn down a job interview, I can't whole-heartedly support the premise.

Every opportunity comes with logistics attached. Should one of this logistics be the fact that you are currently at work or the interview would be during your scheduled work time, I think it could be detrimental to your current employment status should you choose the interview over your work obligation. Postponing, or rescheduling would be prudent.

I guess it also depends on how desperate you are. I really don't like having to respond to someone else's sense of urgency. It can be artificially induced pressure.

Postponing or rescheduling may also serve to illustrate you are an assertive person and may very well work in your favour. Unless of course, they are looking to hire a follower.

If the interview is during a period you are not working... then by all means go for it!

As originally answered on Quora.com.

39. QUESTION: IS IT OKAY TO TELL AN INTERVIEWER THAT YOU ARE NERVOUS?

Answer Provided:

There is no reason you can't tell an interviewer you are nervous, but it serves no purpose other than attempting to reduce your anxiety. It won't!

Any good interviewer will know you are nervous, without you telling them. Depending on their personality, they may understand and be supportive of you or they may use it against you.

You would be better off in trying to reduce your nervousness prior to going for the job interview.

This can be done by brainstorming possible questions you may be asked during the interview and preparing for answers. The job description itself can be a great place to prepare yourself for potential questions.

Another great anxiety-reducing strategy is to do some role playing. Have someone ask you questions and answer them as if you were in the actual job interview.

Anxiety usually won't kill you but seeming overly anxious may kill the interview. You want to come across as being confident and the right person to be hired for the job.

There is an old saying that goes 'fake it until you make it.' If you believe you are confident and not anxious, you in turn will be confident. It really works!

As originally answered on Quora.com.

~

40. QUESTION: I GOT A CALL BACK FOR A JOB INTERVIEW, BUT I TOLD HER I WANTED TO KEEP MY CURRENT JOB. I CHANGED MY MIND. CAN I CALL BACK NOW OR IS IT TOO LATE?

Answer Provided:

Normally I would say "so sad... too bad!" You probably blew the potential opportunity.

The interviewer's initial thought may be "Well, how can I expect you to stick with me if I hire you?"

But then again, they may just say "well here is someone who has the guts to call back."

You might get another chance at an interview, perhaps not. Definitely not, if you don't call back.

One way or another, you need to deal with the ambivalence you seem to be experiencing over your current job. You need some closure. Don't be surprised if you are asked to explain your initial declination of the interview, either on your return phone call or during the interview.

As originally answered on Quora.com.

~

41. QUESTION: HOW CAN YOU PROVE TO AN INTERVIEWER THAT YOU ARE THOUGHTFUL?

Answer Provided:
As in many questions, there is no definitive way to answer it.

Every interviewer has their own set of criteria to decide whether you are thoughtful or not.

Of all the job interviews I have had over the years, I don't think I have ever once asked myself "I wonder if I was thoughtful enough?"

And there is room for interpretation on what the word 'thoughtful' actually means. From my perspective, I think of being thoughtful as bringing an extra cup of coffee back from the coffee machine for my coworker if I was going to grab one. I interpret being thoughtful as thinking of other's needs without the expectation of something in return.

In the instance of a job interview, I think maybe 'thoughtful' isn't the word you are thinking of.

Perhaps you are thinking of being decisive, knowledgeable or well-spoken?

The only way to prove you are all the above ... is to be so.

Even then, it would still be difficult to prove. I suppose the definitive way to know would be you get the job.

A useful technique is to watch the body language of your interviewer. If they seem to be smiling, or drawing closer to you, it might be indicative of whatever you are saying to them is resonating with them. If so, keep it up!

If they seem to be withdrawing from you and frowning, it might be indicative of you're not doing so well. Time to make some adjustments.

As originally answered on Quora.com.

∾

42. QUESTION: SHOULD I GO FOR A JOB INTERVIEW WHEN I'M ALREADY EMPLOYED?

I emailed requesting an interview. I want to explore the opportunity. Should I let them know in my response that I'm currently employed?

I had sent my resume to a company years ago but didn't show up to an interview.

Since then I've worked for a similar company.

They recently emailed me and requested an interview.

I want to explore the opportunity.

Should I respond with a yes and tell them I am currently employed first?

ANSWER PROVIDED:

I wouldn't respond to them and tell them you are currently employed. I don't see the purpose in doing so.

They are either asking you to come in for an interview because they still have you on record as being interested in working for them once upon a time or they have been scouting for talent and think it might be worth their while to bring you into talk to you.

Either way, you are in a good position.

The fact you are currently employed is moot. You may find they have a good offer for you and it's worth your while to move to a new job, or you may find your current job really isn't all bad after-all.

You won't know for sure until you go talk to them.

Just make sure you have updated your resume and have it synced with your Linkedin profile. You can count on the fact the potential employer will be checking you out on-line as you should be them.

As originally answered on Quora.com.

∾

43. QUESTION: WHAT IS THE RIGHT AMOUNT OF TIME TO GET BACK TO AN ORGANIZATION ABOUT YOUR INTERVIEW?

I did the interview back at the end of June and it is now mid-July they said they would contact me by mid to end July, should I just follow up and ask them or no?

ANSWER PROVIDED:

I would call them to see what's up.

No news is no news and they haven't provided you with any.

Job applications are a two-way street, meaning you bring just as much to the table as they do. Sure, they hold all the cards with having the job, but you also took your valuable time to interview with them.

Give them a call and see what's up.

At the worst, you will annoy them and/or they will tell you they gave the job to someone else.

At the best, you may get a job offer for still being interested or perhaps a second interview.

Far too many employers use stalling tactics like this rather than being assertive in telling someone they didn't get the job.

But then again, there may be circumstances preventing them from making a decision until then.

As originally answered on Quora.com.

~

44. QUESTION: IS IT OKAY TO TELL THE INTERVIEWER THAT I'M CURRENTLY HAVING MY OWN BUSINESS?

I quit my job a year back and started a legit small business of my own. The reason being aside from experience, is to fill my time. But I'm having money issue and now trying to apply for a job.

Answer Provided:

I would suggest being prepared to talk about it if the interviewer asks about it.

You may or may not have featured it on your resume. It would depend if the fact you have a small business adds to your experience or skill set and help place you as the ideal candidate for a specific job.

If you have a Linkedin profile, odds are your business will be mentioned there. If you don't have a Linkedin profile and/or your business isn't mentioned there, then perhaps may be one of the root causes of your financial challenges.

If your business is featured on your Linkedin profile, odds are your interviewer will see it. Some job search experts are saying some 93% of hiring managers are checking out social media to see if there are reasons to rule out job applicants.

If it isn't brought up for discussion in the interview, I wouldn't bring it up. If it does, the interviewer might be thinking about conflict of interest issues. Could the business take you away from working on your job or prevent you focusing on what they would be paying you to do?

You will need to develop answers for those types of questions.

It might also be a good time to see how you can make your business more profitable. I know several people who got jobs as a result of their business activities.

As originally answered on Quora.com.

~

45. QUESTION: IS IT APPROPRIATE TO ANSWER "WHY DO YOU WANT THIS JOB?" WITH ANY ANSWER RELATED TO THE MONEY IT PROVIDES OR BEING PAID DURING A JOB INTERVIEW?

Answer Provided:

I'm going to play Devil's Advocate and say 'sure, why not?'

Mentioning the wages and/or benefits are desirable can be an honest way to answer the question. This leads you to follow-up with providing what the job means to you.

You have to craft your answer in a way it aligns what the employer is looking for. They have a problem to solve. You need to be seen as the solution.

This would be where you offer that you like new challenges, you are looking to grow in your career, you believe in the employer is doing and want to be part of it, etc.

As originally answered on Quora.com.

~

46. QUESTION: I HAVE GIVEN SIX INTERVIEWS SO FAR AND I'M CONSTANTLY GETTING REJECTED IN THE FINAL ROUND. WHY IS IT SO?

Answer Provided:

Without ever having seen you in an interview situation, there is no way to answer this question.

But let's turn it by a few degrees and look at it differently.

You are making it to the final rounds of the interview, in at least six situations. While it is depressing you were unsuccessful in landing the job, you must be doing something right in the preliminary interviews to make it that far.

So, what's happening in the final round? Are you getting nervous? Are the interview questions too complicated for you to answer? Do you stumble in answering the questions?

Upon completion of an interview, do you debrief yourself? What went right? What went wrong?

Are there areas you could have benefitted from a 'do over'?

Have you asked any of the interviewers why you were unsuccessful in getting the job. Some people will tell you to never ask that question, others will say 'go for it!' I guess it depends on your comfort level.

You could be doing something that is sabotaging your chances, or it may simply be there are better candidates for the job than you.

All you can do is keep on trying. You should be learning something from every interview. At the very least you will be increasing your job interviewing skills and your self-confidence.

Hopefully, you will be lucky on the next interview. Keep at it!

As originally answered on Quora.com.

~

47. QUESTION: WHAT ARE SOME OF THE BEST WAYS TO DEAL WITH DIFFICULT COLLEAGUES?

Answer Provided:

Your situation, unfortunately, isn't all uncommon.

Over the years, I have studied conflict in the workplace quite a bit.

Here are a couple articles I have written that may provide you some ideas.

Canadian Thistle or Klingon Death Plant: A Gardener's Approach to Managing Workplace Conflict

https://raestonehouse.com/workplace-conflict-resolution/canadian-thistle-or-klingon-death-plant-a-gardener-s-approach-to-managing-workplace-conflict/menu-id-143.html

Workplace conflict is addressed in the second half of the article.

Another one, from my field of healthcare, outlines a case study of bullying in the workplace. **PROtect Yourself! Calley's Story: A Bullying in the Workplace Case Study**

http://raestonehouse.com/workplace-conflict-resolution/protect-yourself-calley-s-story-a-bullying-in-the-workplace-case-study/menu-id-1

48. QUESTION: IS IT OKAY TO NOT HAVE A HARD COPY OF YOUR RESUME WHILE GOING FOR AN INTERVIEW?

Answer Provided:

It isn't a matter of being okay or not okay to have a hard copy of your resume available.

By not having one with you during the interview, you lose out on having a powerful tool at your disposal.

Paper and printing are cheap. Have two copies with you. Have one at the ready should the interviewer have not printed one.

The other one is for your reference. I'm referring to reference in the sense you can use your resume during the interview to illustrate or point out specific points to help you answer interview questions.

In a job interview, presentation and professionalism, while not necessarily scoring points on the interview questions can help bias the way the interview scores your answers.

Having your resume available may show you are serious and professional about obtaining a position with this business.

When it comes to landing the job, when in competition with other candidates with the same qualifications and experience, it might make the difference.

For the sake of a few cent's worth of printing costs, can you afford to take the chance of not having a hard copy of your resume?

As originally answered on Quora.com.

∼

49. QUESTION: HOW DO YOU PREPARE FOR AN INTERVIEW DESCRIBED AS A DEEP DIVE INTO YOUR RESUME AND YOUR DECISION-MAKING SKILLS?

Answer Provided:

You don't indicate whether this is your first interview for a particular job, or if this is a follow-up one.

I would expect if they want to learn more about you and your experience, you are still in the running for the position.

I would also expect a 'deep dive' into your resume would require you to defend or at least explain, the career choices you have made.

It would be kind of like defending your thesis.

The interviewers may agree with your choices or they may disagree with them. But no matter, they were your choices, for better or for worse.

As for defending or explaining your choices, you should be prepared to do so for every career move.

Think as a detective would. Brainstorm a list of questions you would ask someone if you were deep diving into their resume.

Examples:

- Why did you work with XXX company?
- Why did you leave them so soon after starting?
- What skills did you develop there?
- What is your opinion of that business?
- How do you compare this job you are applying for and with the one you have just left?
- What do you hope to gain by working for us?

Once you have developed your list of questions, develop and practice your answers out loud, so you are comfortable with them.

Be aware of any rough spots or areas you might be uncomfortable talking about. Having been fired from a job sometime in the past might be a rough spot. You need to come up with an explanation that mitigates the fact you were fired.

They will probably be judging you on the way you respond to questions, especially if they are testing you 'under fire.' So.... Keep cool!

I hope this helps.

Good luck with your interview.

As originally answered on Quora.com.

~

50. QUESTION: WHAT IS THE EXPECTED ANSWER WHEN ASKED "WHAT'S YOUR OBJECTIVE" IN AN INTERVIEW?

C an I repeat the same line I have written on my resume?

ANSWER PROVIDED:

I'm going to address your second question, first.

Objective statements are out!

According to the so-called experts, don't begin your resumé with an objective statement that describes your desires and career goals.

Today's hiring managers aren't concerned with what is it you're looking for—they're focused on finding the right hire.

This means you need to replace the objective statement with a powerful summary that shows how you will add value to potential employers.

The key is to demonstrate to the reader there is a clear fit between your skills and their needs.

This is where the Summary Statement comes in or what some like to call your "written elevator speech."

Having said that, you still need to be prepared to answer the question in an interview... What's your objective?

I would expect the interviewers would want to hear an honest answer. I would avoid being too honest in saying "I want the big bucks!"

Your answer should tie into how obtaining this position you are applying for fits into your overall career goal. Will it provide personal growth, challenges, opportunities, etc.?

It would be helpful to drop in some comments about how you believe in what the company has been doing well (assuming they are of course) and you want to be part of something bigger than yourself.

As originally answered on Quora.com.

∾

51. QUESTION: HOW CAN I DO WELL IN A JOB INTERVIEW WITH SOCIAL ANXIETY?

Answer Provided:

Having worked most of my career in mental health, some of it as a therapist, I would agree with the comments and suggestions provided by Nancy Barbour.

Social anxiety and any of the other anxiety-related disorders can be debilitating for those who suffer from it. And *suffer* is a good word. Their anxiety sucks out any enjoyment of their life.

I'm going to take a little different approach to answering the question though.

Interviewing for a job is not something we do every day. It is difficult to become self-confident in an activity we are likely performing in a less than an equal capacity with our interviewer.

While social anxiety can certainly be debilitating, not knowing how to perform in a job interview, can produce its own level of stress.

Being self-confident in any endeavour can help reduce anxiety levels, at least to a manageable level.

You would be well-advised to learn how to participate in a job interview. This includes researching the job you are applying for and knowing what the key competencies the employer is looking for.

It also means developing a series of questions the interviewer is likely to ask to assess your capabilities of performing in the role. Role playing answering questions prior to the live version can go a long way in reducing your anxiety.

Fear of the unknown is a common fear. If you practice in advance, you can help reduce your anxiety. Performance anxiety is also common. You are better off to build your confidence in practice sessions before you go live.

Make no mistake. Looking for work is work! You have the added challenge of social anxiety. When you land your job, guess what ... your social anxiety will still be there and will probably affect your day-to-day working conditions.

That's where the psychotherapy comes in.

Good luck in overcoming this challenge. You can do it!

As originally answered on Quora.com.

∾

52. QUESTION: HOW SHOULD I ANSWER THE QUESTION "TELL ME MORE ABOUT YOURSELF" IN A JOB INTERVIEW?

Answer Provided:

Focus on the aspects of your *work experience* that apply specifically to the position you're applying for.

This can also take the form of, "if I asked one of your faculty members/previous supervisors to tell me about you, what would they say?"

Your answer should spotlight the education, experience, and work ethic matches what the employer is seeking in an employee. End by saying you are *well prepared* for the position the interviewer is trying to fill.

This would also be a good opportunity to reiterate your Summary Statement from your resume. This is where you are able to promote yourself as the ideal candidate for the job.

~

53. QUESTION: IS IT MORAL WHEN COMPANIES POST FAKE JOBS ON CAREER WEBSITES FOR THE PURPOSE OF PRE-QUALIFYING PEOPLE WITHOUT ACTUALLY NEEDING NEW STAFF SINCE THAT'S A BIG WASTE OF TIME FOR THOSE WHO SEEK EMPLOYMENT?

Answer Provided:

A problem with ethics is it isn't always a black & white situation. Many ethical situations are grey at best.

I would expect, while posting jobs that don't exist isn't common place, neither is it unknown. I'm sure some companies do it as their standard practice.

Years ago, I applied for a job that looked quite interesting. I must have had the qualifications as they invited me in for an interview. The interview seemed to be going well when they asked me if I was willing to relocate to another city in our province. I said 'no' as I had just moved my family across the country to the city we were in and didn't want to go through that process again.

The interview seemed to fizzle out after that. I believe this to be a 'bait and switch' scenario. I wonder if there actually was a local job or if the interview was bait to hire people for other hard to fill positions in other cities?

I know of another situation where a nurse colleague was interviewed for the position of the Administrator for a Hospice House. It became apparent to her during the interview the position had already been filled and they were going through the motions of interviewing several candidates to make the hiring process look legitimate. That was a waste of time.

There is another way to look at the situation though. While it doesn't necessarily give you an immediate job, it can be beneficial to be pre-qualified in the event something does open up. There are also benefits to being interviewed by the business. If and when a second interview results, you will have a better idea as to what the interview would be like.

As originally answered on Quora.com.

54. QUESTION: WHAT ARE SOME THINGS YOU SHOULD, AND SHOULD NOT SAY, DURING A JOB INTERVIEW WHEN YOU GET ASKED "SO TELL ME A LITTLE BIT ABOUT YOURSELF?"

Answer Provided:

Focus on the aspects of your *work experience* that apply specifically to the position you're applying for.

This can also take the form of, "if I asked one of your faculty members/previous supervisors to tell me about you, what would they say?"

Your answer should spotlight the education, experience, and work ethic matches what the employer is seeking in an employee.

End by saying you are *well prepared* for the position the interviewer is trying to fill.

Another version of 'tell me about yourself' is… **"What would you like me to know about you?"**

Keep the answer *short* and *power-packed*.

Identify four to five qualities that make you a strong candidate.

Highlight your academic achievements, ability to do the type of work you are interviewing for, and your work ethic.

55. QUESTION: HOW DO I GET A JOB WITHOUT LYING ABOUT MYSELF?

Answer Provided:

Benjamin, as you are only 19 years old, I'm going to make the assumption that what you are really asking is "How can I get a job without having any skills or experience?"

If I'm wrong, sorry … perhaps somebody else may benefit from my response.

Lying, will work against you, not for you. The only one you will be fooling, will be yourself.

Assertions of skills, experiences gained and employment can easily be verified or debunked. Any skilled interviewer will see through a job candidate that is lying.

I would expect at 19 years old, you don't have a lot to capitalize on in your resume. That's not necessarily a problem. Everybody has to start somewhere.

You have some work ahead of you. I would suggest a two-pronged approach, developing your resume as well as your Linkedin profile. They should resonate with each other.

One of the first steps is to take an inventory of the skills and experience you actually have. This can include any summer or part-time jobs you have held. Brainstorm a list of duties and skills you had and developed while in those jobs.

Unless you have developed some specialized skills, you will likely be looking at an entry-level job. Most of us go through this process. It is only by trying different jobs can we determine what we don't want to do for a job and what we might like to do.

Take advantage of this time in your life and explore possibilities until you determine what you are passionate about.

I graduated high school with little work experience and the passion to become a chef. After three years cooking in a large institutional kitchen, I decided while I enjoyed cooking, I didn't want to cook for a living. I looked for opportunities available to me and decided on becoming a Registered Nurse. I have been doing that for over 40 years.

While working as a nurse, I developed many other skills that have helped me throughout my life.

I've learned my passion in life wasn't cooking, it hasn't been working as a nurse, but it has been in helping other people.

As you go through life you will collect experiences, skills, stories and self-confidence to share them with others and you will find lying isn't necessary. Just be yourself.

As originally answered on Quora.com.

∾

56. QUESTION: IF YOU SERVED TIME FOR SOMETHING YOU DIDN'T DO, WOULD YOU MENTION THAT IN ANY JOB INTERVIEWS?

Answer Provided:

Yes, no, maybe... it depends!

If you have served time i.e. you were charged for a criminal offence in a court of law and were incarcerated for a period it is a fact of life ... your life. You can't hide it. The important aspect of it is you have hopefully come out a better person, and you learned from the experience.

I don't think you should necessarily be volunteering this information in a job interview but on the other hand neither should you be ignoring it.

These type of situations can come up in an interview when the Interviewer is looking at your resume and wondering about an unexplained absence from the workforce.

You need to have practiced an answer for that particular question. It may also be phrased in a different way. The question of 'would you pass a criminal record check?' might be a way it is posed to you. If you are not truthful or evasive, it will work against you.

For some jobs, where a criminal record check is required, the fact you served time, would be revealed.

While you can control how you present the details of your wrongful conviction and subsequent incarceration, you have no control of how the interviewer receives it and processes it.

Perhaps they regularly hire convicted felons who have served their debt to society. It may not be a big deal to them. For others, the fact you have been locked up may be a deal breaker. They could terminate the interview on the spot.

The fact you say you were wrongfully charged, doesn't come into play in a job interview. However, it remains as an obstacle for you to overcome and move past. The past doesn't necessarily equal the future and you have your whole life ahead of you to right the wrong.

Best of luck to you!

As originally answered on Quora.com.

∾

57. QUESTION: IS IT POSSIBLE TO BE TOO SURE OF YOURSELF?

Answer Provided:
I believe it is quite possible.

Being sure of yourself is a combination of having a healthy ego, a strong self-confidence and a broad range of experience to apply to different situations.

Many of us can be quite sure of ourselves in certain areas, perhaps public speaking as an example, but not so secure in other areas such as networking.

Skills and confidence in one specific area don't necessarily cross-over to other areas.

There are people who are narcissistic and have an inflated view of their self-worth and their abilities. They can't fathom the idea they aren't perfect in all aspects of their life.

Then there are those 'that are so far behind, they think they are first.' They don't know what they don't know. We often call that 'delusions of adequacy.'

The Universe has a way of levelling things out. Being too sure of oneself a few times may work out, but perhaps not the next time.

As originally answered on Quora.com.

~

58. QUESTION: WHAT ADVICE CAN YOU GIVE TO SOMEONE WITH SOCIAL ANXIETY, IN REGARDS TO JOB SEARCHING PROSPECTS?

Answer Provided:

Your question touches on two areas I have personally experienced and have spent a great deal of time researching strategies to overcome.

In my e-book**Power Networking for Shy People: Tips & Techniques for Moving from Shy to Sly!**I outline strategies for shy networkers to level the playing field with those who are more outgoing.

Shyness and social anxiety are the same thing. We weren't born with it; we learned it. If we learned it, we can learn other techniques of overcoming or at least working within our anxiety and making it manageable.

A big part of how we experience social anxiety is what is called a 'self-fulfilling prophesy.'

We are expecting to be anxious as we have in the past. So, what happens? We become anxious because we always have in the past. We are talking about fear.

A commonly used acronym for FEAR is false expectations appearing real. That is the self-fulfilling prophesy in action.

When it comes to job searching and interviewing, it can often play havoc with our insecurities and increasing our social anxieties.

Many people believe the employer holds all the power in a hiring situation and it is an unfair balance of power. This in turn increases our insecurities.

I believe knowledge is power and if you have it, you can increase your success rate.

That lead me to write and publish**You're Hired! Job Search Strategies That Work.** As the title says, I provide strategies to increase your personal power in the job searching process. The knowledge will help you gain the power to be effective in your job search.

Both increasing your knowledge of job searching and becoming more comfortable in social situations takes time.

When it comes to social anxiety specific to job searching, it is likely related to the prospect of having to do cold calling i.e. to people you don't know, obtaining references and/or worrying about the idea of having to answer interview questions. At least it was for me.

I would be remiss if I didn't mention one of the best ways to reduce your social anxiety and in turn increase your self-confidence and the likelihood of landing a job, is to join Toastmasters.

As a 24-year member, I can't speak highly enough of the benefits and person growth I have seen in myself and countless others. Check to see if there is a club in your community.

As originally answered on Quora.com.

～

59. QUESTION: WHEN A COMPANY ASKS FOR REFERENCES WITH ADDRESSES, DO YOU INCLUDE THE PERSON'S HOME ADDRESS, OR THEIR WORK ADDRESS?

Answer Provided:

One of the necessary preliminary activities prior to going for a job interview is lining up a team of references.

These references should represent both personal and business-related.

You should determine in advance how your references want to be contacted by a potential employer following up on your behalf.

Make it easy for both your references and the employer. Your references should be readily accessible. So, while one may prefer their business contact be used, another may prefer to use their home contact info.

As originally answered on Quora.com.

~

60. QUESTION: WHAT ARE TIPS AND TRICKS TO INCREASE YOUR ODDS OF GETTING A JOB AT A COMPANY BY USING NETWORKING SKILLS?

A nswer Provided:

I would suggest utilizing a multi-faceted approach.

Firstly, research the company on-line. Locate and read their social media properties. More than likely they will have a Facebook business page, a Linkedin Business page and possibly a Twitter profile.

Find out what is important to the company. What do they believe in? What is important to them? What are they most proud of?

Secondly, find out who the key people behind the company are. What roles do they take on in the company? Then check out their individual profiles on Linkedin.

If you are comfortable in doing so, send them an invitation to connect on Linkedin and provide them with a reason they might want to connect. Not the fact you are looking for a job though.

If the company's social media properties allow for posting comments, see how you can add value by posting replies to their postings.

Networking face-to-face with people in hiring positions in companies can be a little tricky, in most cases, their networking is restricted to events with other members of the company.

There can be a benefit in leveraging your connections to see if anybody knows anyone working at the company in question, or if they have any connections there.

If you are gutsy, you may want to contact somebody in the company for an informational chat where you ask for the opportunity to pick their brain.

In business networking events, it can be helpful to ask people you connect with outright "Do you know anybody who works at….?

I go into strategies such as these in greater detail in my book on job search strategies that work.

As originally answered on Quora.com.

～

61. **QUESTION: HOW CAN I ASK FOR MY JOB BACK AFTER GETTING FIRED? I LIKED THE JOB AND WAS SUCCESSFUL THERE FOR 20 MONTHS BUT LOST MY TEMPER AND USED EXPLETIVES WHILE ON A CALL WITH TECH SUPPORT LAST WEEK.**

This was the only time this has ever happened.

Answer Provided:

If you have the courage to do so... do so!

Your question leaves a lot to the imagination.

Were you in a unionized job?

Was there a disciplinary meeting?

Was progressive discipline offered before the firing?

I don't see anything in your question and supplementary information to say you were sorry for what you did, or you learned something from the situation.

Sure, you can ask for your old job back, but why should they give it to you?

Are you aware whether your comments did any damage to the business?

Did you do anything at the time to mitigate the potential damage or loss of faith in the company you likely created?

I have been fired before and was successful in getting a job back, not the original one though. I had a union behind me that backed me up.

When you are on your own ... you are on your own.

I would say it is time to move on. You may want to polish up your resume and find some credible references to get you past the having been fired hurdle.

As originally answered on Quora.com.

~

62. QUESTION: I HAVE GIVEN SIX INTERVIEWS SO FAR AND I'M CONSTANTLY GETTING REJECTED IN THE FINAL ROUND. WHY IS IT SO?

A nswer Provided:

Without ever having seen you in an interview situation, there is no way to answer this question.

But let's turn it by a few degrees and look at it differently.

You are making it to the final rounds of the interview, in at least six situations. While it is depressing you were unsuccessful in landing the job, you must be doing something right in the preliminary interviews to make it that far.

So, what's happening in the final round? Are you getting nervous? Are the interview questions too complicated for you to answer? Do you stumble in answering the questions?

Upon completion of an interview, do you debrief yourself? What went right? What went wrong?

Are there areas you could have benefitted from a 'do over'?

Have you asked any of the interviewers why you were unsuccessful in getting the job. Some people will tell you to never ask that question, others will say 'go for it!' I guess it depends on your comfort level.

You could be doing something that is sabotaging your chances, or it may simply be there are better candidates for the job than you.

All you can do is keep on trying. You should be learning something from every interview. At the very least you will be increasing your job interviewing skills and your self-confidence.

Hopefully, you will be lucky on the next interview. Keep at it!

As originally answered on Quora.com.

~

63. QUESTION: HOW DO YOU BECOME CONFIDENT IF YOU ARE A VERY SHY PERSON?

A nswer Provided:

You ask a short simple question that requires a complex answer to do it justice.

It's far too easy for people who don't experience being shy and quiet to say 'just stop doing it.'

Life doesn't work that way.

Being shy and quiet is merely a manifestation of having a deficit of social skills and a lack of self-confidence in the area of socializing.

If you experience severe anxiety over the thought of getting out there and socializing, it would be a different matter.

Being shy and quiet is a temporary state. You can change it.

The first step of course is being open to making changes in your life. Learning to socialize better does require socializing more.

It can be helpful to go to social events with a more outgoing person. They can introduce you to people and you might be able to emulate the skills they possess when it comes to socializing.

Think of improving your social skills as a series of incremental steps. Each step you take should be evaluated and adjusted as needed.

I would suggest creating your own plan for socialization. It could be something as simple as talking to a stranger at the bus stop or while in line at a store.

It could be in participating in a 1 to 1 conversation at a networking session when somebody asks you a question. It could work up to your initiating the conversation.

One cure for being quiet, is actually having something to say. It can be helpful to be up-to-date on what is happening in your community or even the larger picture of your country.

As well as speaking or talking about a topic you know about, it can be equally valuable in being a good listener. Asking questions to a person who is telling you a story can make you a great conversationalist in the eyes of the story-teller.

Assuming you are over the age of 18, I would be remiss if I didn't mention the value of joining a Toastmasters club in your community. As a member you will help develop your communication skills, which in turn develops your self-confidence. It can be a great way to overcome your quiet, shy ways. It has worked for me.

~

64. QUESTION: I'M SHY SO I AM NOT ABLE TO SAY SORRY OR EXPRESS MYSELF IN MY VIEWPOINTS. IS IT WRONG TO BE AN INTROVERT?

Answer Provided:

The concept of right or wrong is often in the eyes of the beholder. Being an introvert is neither right nor wrong.

What is wrong, at least in my opinion, is being shy as well as an introvert, not being happy about it and not doing anything to rectify the situation.

In my mind that is a waste of human potential.

Simply put, shyness is a lack of communication and social skills.

Shyness can be a self-fulfilling prophesy. We are afraid of socializing and conversing with others, so we isolate ourselves. We avoid conversation. This in turns increases our fear. Then we isolate ourselves and our fear increases.

We can break the cycle if we choose to. It takes time and effort. It takes stepping way out of our comfort zones.

Assuming you are over the age of 18, I would suggest you look to see if there is a Toastmasters club in your area.

While Toastmasters doesn't specifically have a program that focuses on reducing shyness, almost all the activities serve to incrementally increase your self-confidence.

Increasing your self-confidence is the key to reducing one's shyness.

If you are an introvert, you will be one for the rest of your life. That is how you are hard-wired.

Embrace your introversion!

As originally answered on Quora.com.

∼

65. QUESTION: HOW SHOULD I LIST AN EMPLOYMENT GAP OF 7 YEARS ON MY CV?

Answer Provided:

As has been suggested, you shouldn't draw attention to the fact you haven't been in the workforce for 7 years.

However, you definitely need to be prepared to answer a question about it, should you get to a job interview.

At the very least, the interviewer may be curious. At the most, they are doing their due diligence.

While there are numerous reasons a person may be out of the workforce for a length of time, all valid, it does raise one's curiosity. Many would wonder if there has been a lengthy prison term involved.

It also depends on if this is the first job you are seeking after the gap or if you have had other jobs since then. If you have had other jobs since the gap, it is likely moot.

If you are coming off of the seven-year gap, you will likely need to mitigate the effect it has on your employability.

When you were off, did you do any training or any activities that would add to your skills or experience?

Not knowing what field or profession you were working in before you were off, I'm left wondering if your former work experience and skills are relevant? You may need to be prepared to have to defend and promote the value of your previous work experience if it is relevant to a job you are applying for.

As originally answered on Quora.com.

~

66. QUESTION: IS NOT BEING ACTIVE ON SOCIAL MEDIA BAD FOR JOB-SEEKERS?

Answer Provided:

It's not necessarily bad for you, but it isn't good either.

Recent articles on job searching are saying some 93% of employers are researching applicants online to see what their digital footprint is. Often, they are doing so even before calling you for an interview.

They are looking to get a sense of your character. Basically, they want to see if you fit into their tribe. They want to rule you out or in before they contact you.

Being active on social media isn't likely the most important issue. It is the content you are sharing that could be problematic. If you are sharing photos of you getting hammered on your vacation or at parties, it doesn't shed you in a good light as a future employee. It doesn't help any either if you have 'friends' who are tagging you in compromising situations.

Conversely, not being active on social media, or having a social media presence at all can also work against you. The employer may assume you are not very good at technical matters or have paranoid tendencies.

The other caveat is it really depends on what industry you are working in and your age demographic.

A proactive social media presence would be an expectation in a younger job seeker but not so in an older worker. Unless the older worker was seeking work as a communications director or in the marketing field.

As originally answered on Quora.com.

67. QUESTION: HOW DO I ADDRESS BEING FIRED FROM A PREVIOUS JOB IN A RESUME, ON AN APPLICATION, AND INTERVIEWS?

Answer Provided:

Unless the interviewer personally knows you, or knows of your situation, it isn't likely to come up in an interview, unless you draw attention to the fact.

If you are applying for work within the same company, likely there will be documentation on your personnel record.

The challenge is you may have to be prepared to explain an absence from the workforce, as identified in your resume, if it took you a while to get another job. Or if the one you are applying for is the next one since you got fired.

In the off chance you are asked about your 'firing' you can minimalize its negative effect by having a story prepared in advance. The 'why' you got terminated may not be as important as what you learned from the situation.

The last time I got fired, I used the time to upgrade my skills in interpersonal conflict resolution, assertiveness and interpersonal communication. I became a stronger personality as a result of being fired.

Another aspect to address is how you feel about being fired. Being fired can shake you up for a while. The important thing I personally learned was while the employer can take my job but they can't take my dignity. As you travel through life, you may very well get fired. It happens. But life goes on.

As originally answered on Quora.com.

~

68. QUESTION: HOW LONG SHOULD I WAIT FOR CONTACT FROM AN EMPLOYER DURING THE HIRING PROCESS?

Answer Provided:

I would definitely contact them.

They have an obligation to you. An agreement for employment has been made.

Perhaps there is a snag with the process. Even if it is a major problem, you should still be in the loop.

I feel it is better to be considered a nuisance at their end if you call than to be worrying about not having any information at your end.

As originally answered on Quora.com.

∽

69. QUESTION: WHAT DO JOB SEEKERS MOST DISLIKE ABOUT THE JOB SEARCH PROCESS IN AMERICA TODAY?

Answer Provided:

I'm going to expand the question to include all of North America, which includes Canada as it is where I reside.

From my perspective, the biggest complaint I hear from job searchers is it is an unfair relationship.

From their perspective, it seems the employer, or whoever is interviewing them, has all the power. They know the interview questions in advance and they know the answers they are looking for.

Some interviewers have advanced people skills, others are way out of their comfort zones and make it very uncomfortable for the job searcher. If you are interviewing and you don't get the feeling you are wanted there, it is difficult to do your best in the interview.

Another complaint I hear from job searchers is they apply for a job, possibly get interviewed but they never get any follow-up.

I understand for some jobs, there can be a landslide of applications. Issuing a statement such as 'due to the high volume of applicants expected for this position, we will only be contacting select ones for follow-up', while understandable, in my view is poor public relations.

The organization is missing an opportunity to develop a relationship with the job searcher for future hiring possibilities.

From the job searchers perspective, they sit and wait for an acknowledgement. They don't even know if their application was received by the organization.

Powerlessness, is the biggest complaint I hear about from job searchers and I have experienced it myself.

As originally answered on Quora.com.

∾

70. QUESTION: WHAT ARE SOME TIPS TO NOT BE NERVOUS FOR A BUSINESS PRESENTATION?

Answer Provided:

While it has been suggested being nervous is good, I'm going to challenge that thought by disagreeing.

Self-confidence is better than being nervous any day.

Using poker as an example, a pair of aces beats a pair of kings. Self-confidence beats nervousness.

There are at least three issues that need to be addressed in answering this question:

1. Fear of public speaking i.e. nervousness

2. Fear of failure

3. Intimidation by the audience

All three of these issues are interconnected.

Nervousness can be caused by lack of self-confidence, poor public speaking skills, being affected by past public speaking situations that didn't go well, etc. Don't underestimate the effect that too much caffeine in the system can have in increasing your nervousness.

Becoming less fearful and proficient at public speaking is achievable. It takes time and a concerted effort to move forward but is well within the reach of everyone.

Consider joining a local Toastmasters club if you have one nearby. At a Toastmasters club you will learn to speak in varying situations that require public speaking confidence. A business presentation isn't really any different from any other presentation other than the fact that there may be repercussions to your career or salary if you don't do well.

Fear of failure can become a self-fulfilling prophesy. If you go into the business presentation from a position of weakness i.e. you think the audience is better than you and perhaps you aren't worthy to be there, odds are that is how you are going to present yourself.

While your audience can be intimidating, I think it is important to keep in mind your audience may be somewhat intimidated by you as well. After all, if they act upon your proposal or conversely, they don't, it may have repercussions for their career as well.

Now back to the nervousness in the short term. There are steps you can take to significantly reduce your nervousness and improve your presentation's effectiveness.

1. Know your presentation/material inside out.

2. Be prepared for FAQs (frequently asked questions). If the questions aren't asked, insert them into your presentation.

3. Practice your presentation out loud. Recording yourself on video can be effective in helping you become comfortable with your content. The downside of practicing alone is you don't have the advantage a live audience brings e.g. feedback, attention etc.

4. The Wonder Woman super pose works for some people in advance to going to your presentation. Personally, I would feel stupid doing so. Far better to envision your success.

5. Athletes use envisioning success as part of their daily training. If it works for them, it will work for you as a presenter. Prior to your live presentation, any time you think about your presentation think about it in positive terms. See yourself being successful and achieving your purpose. Think of happy smiling faces hanging on every word you say. Envision yourself wowing them.

6. Upon completion of a business presentation debrief yourself. What worked? What didn't work? And then factor in what you learned about yourself for a better presentation next time.

ABOUT THE AUTHOR

Rae A. Stonehouse is a Canadian born author & speaker.

His professional career as a Registered Nurse working predominantly in psychiatry/mental health, has spanned four decades.

Rae has embraced the principal of CANI (Constant and Never-ending Improvement) as promoted by thought leaders such as Tony Robbins and brings that philosophy to each of his publications and presentations.

Rae has dedicated the latter segment of his journey through life to overcoming his personal inhibitions. As a 25+ year member of Toast-masters International he has systematically built his self-confidence and communicating ability. He is passionate about sharing his lessons with his readers and listeners.

His publications thus far are of the self-help, self-improvement genre and systematically offer valuable sage advice on a specific topic.

His writing style can be described as being conversational. As an author, Rae strives to have a one-to-one conversation with each of his readers, very much like having your own personal self-development coach.

Rae is known for having a wry sense of humour that features in his publications. To learn more about Rae A. Stonehouse, visit the Wonderful World of Rae Stonehouse at http://raestonehouse.com.

facebook.com/rae.stonehouse

twitter.com/raestonehouse

PUBLICATIONS BY THE AUTHOR

Power Networking for Shy People: Tips & Techniques for Moving from Shy to Sly!

http://powernetworkingforshypeople.com

∼

PROtect Yourself! Empowering Tips & Techniques for Personal Safety: A Practical Violence Prevention Manual for Healthcare Workers http://protectyourselfnow.ca/

∼

E=Emcee Squared: Tips & Techniques to Becoming a Dynamic Master of Ceremonies

http://emceesquared.mremcee.com/

∼

Power of Promotion: On-line Marketing for Toastmasters Club Growth http://powerofpromotion.ca/

∾

You're Hired! Job Search Strategies That Work (This is the complete program)

E-book & Paperback: https://books2read.com/yourehired

On-line E-course: http://liveforexcellenceacademy.com/

(Available as a self-directed or instructor-led program)

∾

You're Hired! Resume Tactics: Job Search Strategies That Work

E-book & Paperback: https://books2read.com/resumetactics

On-line E-course: http://liveforexcellenceacademy.com/

∾

Job Interview Preparation: Job Search Strategies That Work

E-book& Paperback: books2read.com/jobinterviewpreparation

On-line E-course: http://liveforexcellenceacademy.com/

∾

You're Hired! Leveraging Your Network: Job Search Strategies That Work

E-book & Paperback: http://books2read.com/leveragingyournetwork

On-line E-course: http://liveforexcellenceacademy.com/

∾

You're Hired! Power Tactics: Job Search Strategies That Work (This is a box set containing the complete content of Resume Tactics, Job Interview Preparation & Leveraging Your Network)

E-book: http://books2read.com/powertactics

∾

If you have found this book and program to be helpful, please leave us a warm review wherever you purchased this book.

www.ingramcontent.com/pod-product-compliance
Lightning Source LLC
Chambersburg PA
CBHW071205210326
41597CB00016B/1679